REVOLUTIONARY STRATEGIES

of the
FOUNDING FATHERS

Leadership Lessons from America's Most Successful Patriots

SCOTT THORPE

SOURCEBOOKS, INC.
NAPERVILLE, ILLINOIS

Published by Sourcebooks, Inc.
P.O. Box 4410, Naperville, Illinois 60567-4410
(630) 961-3900
FAX: (630) 961-2168
www.sourcebooks.com

Library of Congress Cataloging-in-Publication Data

Thorpe, Scott.
  Revolutionary strategies : leadership lessons from America's most successful patriots / by Scott Thorpe.
      p. cm.
  Includes bibliographical references and index.
  ISBN 1-57071-934-9 (alk. paper)
  1. Statesmen—United States—History—18th century. 2. Revolutionaries—United States—History—18th century. 3. United States—Politics and government—1775-1783. 4. United States—History—Revolution, 1775-1783. 5. Leadership—United States—Case studies. 6. Businessmen—United States—History. 7. Inventors—United States—History. 8. Management—United States—Case studies. 9. Success in business—United States—Case studies. I. Title.
  E210 .T485 2003
  658.4'092—dc21

Printed and bound in the United States of America
VHG 10 9 8 7 6 5 4 3 2 1

To all the revolutionaries who had the courage to build a better world

Acknowledgments

Thanks to the staff at Cowpens National Battlefield and Gloria Henry at the John Dickinson Plantation for aiding my research. I am grateful to the staffs of the J. Willard Marriot, Kaysville City, Weber County, and Salt Lake County Libraries for keeping me well-supplied with books and reference materials.

Table of Contents

✦ ✦ ✦

REVOLUTIONARY
STRATEGIES
of the
FOUNDING FATHERS

CHAPTER ONE

THE ESSENTIAL REVOLUTION

The Masters of Revolution

Is life so dear, or peace so sweet, as to be purchased
at the price of chains and slavery?
Forbid it, Almighty God! I know not what course
others may take; but as for me,
give me liberty or give me death!

—PATRICK HENRY

Learning from History's Greatest Revolutionaries

In today's competitive business climate, revolution is essential to survival. Global economics, technological advances, and industry consolidation are changing the competitive environment at an accelerating pace, putting even the most successful businesses at risk. A quick look at some of the Nifty Fifty companies from the early 1970s highlights the need for continuing change. All were admired leaders with strong market positions and earnings. But even these pillars of the American economy had to revolutionize their business models or see their fortunes decline amid waves of competitive innovation.

- **AT&T**—Local phone business and equipment business divested. Strong competition in long-distance service shrinks profits.
- **Coca-Cola**—Enormous growth outside of North America.
- **Disney**—Vertical integration into media distribution.
- **General Electric Co.**—Massive restructuring. The bulk of profits are now from finance, rather than producing industrial products.
- **IBM**—Massive downsizing in 1980s. De-emphasized core mainframe business while growing profitable service business.
- **McDonald's**—Aggressively growing in places that hadn't heard of fries and a shake thirty years ago.
- **Philip Morris**—Strategy is still profitable, but the profits are going to the plaintiffs.
- **Polaroid**—Filed for bankruptcy.
- **Texas Instruments**—Corporate focus on new digital signal processing technology. Most businesses that were producing revenue in the 1970s were sold or closed.
- **Xerox**—Nimbler, cheaper competitors dominate the market.

Because revolution is inescapable, those leading modern upheavals can learn much from history's most successful revolutionaries, the Founding Fathers of the United States. The Founding Fathers succeeded despite enormous philosophical differences and massive egos, winning an impossible war and then creating new forms of government that changed the world. Their lessons are applicable from the boardrooms of multinational corporations to the garage office suites of struggling start-ups.

The American Revolution was audacious. A future American nation may have been inevitable, but in the 1700s, the founding of a republic from Britain's American colonies was inconceivable. Britain was America's best customer. The colonies enjoyed many advantages as an integral part of the world's most sophisticated economy. Colonists considered independence undesirable and knew a rebellion would never succeed.

Britain was the superpower of the late eighteenth century. The Royal Navy ruled the oceans. Its guns could level most American cities or stop colonial commerce. If that wasn't deterrent enough, the British were capable of landing large, professional armies anywhere in the colonies. They had an overwhelming advantage in numbers, equipment, and experience. And the British military was supported by the world's best financial and industrial infrastructure.

Against the British military juggernaut, the colonies started with almost nothing. They had no central government. The Continental Congress had little formal authority and could not tax. The colonies had no armies, just poorly trained, unreliable militia without enough money, powder, or experienced officers.

Even if the colonies were able to beat the British, it was unlikely that they could have created a republic spanning the thirteen colonies. Democracy had only succeeded on a limited scale in city-states. Getting citizens to cooperate when separated by thousands of miles seemed impossible. Colonies were more different than alike. Southern aristocrats, New England traders, and mid-Atlantic farmers distrusted and disliked each other, making a United States of America as improbable then as a United States of Asia seems today.

Despite these obstacles, the Founding Fathers succeeded. By following their example, you too can thrive in difficult, changing times.

Ongoing Revolution

Man is born free, and everywhere
he is in chains.

—JEAN JACQUES ROUSSEAU

Change is coming to your industry

The American Revolution was part of a series of interrelated changes that began in England more than a century earlier. The English Parliament issued *The Petition of Right* in 1628, claiming freedom from taxation without parliamentary consent or the forcible quartering of troops, issues that would later be central to the American Revolution. The English Civil War, beginning in 1642, deposed Charles I and established the rule of Parliament. Parliament deposed another king, James II, in the Glorious Revolution of 1688, and issued its *Bill of Rights* specifying its powers. These political reforms enabled industrial innovation. Newcome's steam engine began pumping water from coal mines in 1712. The spinning jenny that automated thread production was patented in 1769. Protection from taxation, internal free trade, and commerce with North America and Asia were turning Britain into the world's first industrial power.

Change begat more change. America and France followed with their own rebellions for political and economic liberty, spawning revolutions that have reverberated throughout the world, touching all aspects of life: agriculture, science, families, religion, culture, politics, and business. And change hasn't slowed—it accelerates with each generation.

Even institutions that have been through repeated revolutions will have them again. In the 1960s, steel was one of the world's mature industries. But Nucor Corporation—then a joist fabricator—needed to reduce the cost of its steel to compete. So it built the first steel mini-mill, producing steel from scrap in a small operation instead of from ore at a massive foundry. Nucor's revolution was so successful that they are now the largest steel producer in the United States. A revolution is coming to your business, even if you just finished the last one.

Reluctant Revolutionaries

All great changes are irksome to the human mind, especially those which are attended with great dangers and uncertain effects.

—JOHN ADAMS,
IN A LETTER TO JAMES WARREN, APRIL 22, 1776

The Seeds of Rebellion

The Founders were reluctant revolutionaries. Like most Americans, they had been contented British subjects. The colonies prospered on the periphery of the British Empire, lightly governed and lightly taxed. American ships enjoyed the extensive protection of British naval and commercial power while the British army protected settlements from the French and Spanish. Colonists appreciated the liberal rights granted them as British subjects. And they had no trouble evading or ignoring British laws that they did not like, such as customs duties.

Of this contented group, the Founders were generally the most contented of all. They were making fortunes taking advantage of limitless opportunities of the Americas under the protection of British commercial and military power. Benjamin Franklin was one of the satisfied, loyal subjects of King George. Franklin ran away from his Boston apprenticeship to seek his fortune in the booming city of Philadelphia. A smart businessman, he became rich admonishing Americans to live modest, frugal lives in his *Poor Richard's Almanack*. He expanded that fortune by acting as a colonial agent, enjoying life in England for most of the years leading up to the Revolution.

Like other Americans, Franklin only reluctantly became a revolutionary when the British tried to change things. The catalyst was the Seven Years' War, 1754–1763. The Seven Years' War, or French and Indian War as it is often called in the United States, was a global war fought between Britain and France and their allies. The ambitious young George Washington won one of the first skirmishes of the war before later being defeated and captured himself. France prevailed early on in the war. But after William Pitt became prime minister, the British secured a series of pivotal victories. The British took control of Canada, parts of India, and solidified their dominance around the world.

Britain accumulated a massive debt from the war. But because raising taxes at home had proved deadly to English kings, King George III sought other sources of revenue to balance the budget. George's ministers noted that the prosperous American colonies were very lightly taxed. Since the colonies now enjoyed greater security because of the war, the ministers reasoned it would be fair to increase their tax burden. Prime Minister George Greenville imposed duties known as the Greenville Acts on a range of imports, and he directed royal officials to collect duties and catch smugglers. Until then, tax collectors cost the Crown several times what they collected because of smuggling and evasion.

Greenville's impositions were not well-received. The Seven Years' War made the colonies feel less dependent on Britain. With the French gone, the colonies didn't need British protection and didn't want their taxes. Colonial merchants were all smugglers, so the British crackdown threatened the whole American economy. When royal officials tried to collect duties or seize contraband goods, merchants and their friends reacted with violence. Tax collectors were intimidated into inaction or physically prevented from carrying out the law. Americans organized boycotts against British imports. Local courts threw out the smuggling cases that went to trial while smugglers successfully sued British officials for carrying out their duties.

His Majesty's government was shocked that its modest sharing of the costs of empire were received in such a treasonous fashion. It retaliated in 1765 with the Quartering Act and the Stamp Act, requiring colonists to pay for the support of British troops and directly taxing official documents. Colonial legislatures were threatened with dissolution if they didn't provide funds to quarter troops. Influential colonial merchants and lawyers faced crippling direct taxation on their livelihood. These demands were made even more onerous because new British restrictions on colonial currency had caused an American recession. Facing impoverishment and ruin, Americans began to realize they must change their relationship with the mother country or have their prosperity wrecked. Many loyal British subjects, such as Benjamin Franklin, reluctantly became revolutionaries.

We naturally try to avoid change, but the world does not always allow us that option. Often we must start our own revolutions or be swept up in someone else's.

IBM experienced a reluctant revolution in the 1980s and early 1990s. "Big Blue" had dominated numerous lucrative markets. Many saw the Department of Justice as its only serious competition. And then the world changed. Plummeting computing costs spawned a legion of hungry new competitors. Even key suppliers like Microsoft and Intel became competitive threats. Soon mighty IBM was engulfed in revolution. Its business models and even its cherished culture became obsolete in a matter of years. IBM had two options: fade away or mount its own revolution. It chose revolution, restructuring its business from selling mainframes and hardware to supplying software and services. Revolution is inevitable. You might as well lead the next one yourself.

Good Revolutions

I hold it that a little rebellion now and then
is a good thing.

—THOMAS JEFFERSON

Revolution is Progress

While many of the Founders reluctantly became revolutionaries, others welcomed the opportunity. Revolution was their chance for success. Henry Knox was trapped selling books in Boston. The rebellion allowed him to escape his shop, becoming one of Washington's most trusted generals and later Secretary of War. Englishman Thomas Paine had always been a rebel. A failed pirate, smuggler, merchant, and tax collector, he wrote a modest pamphlet that brought him to the attention of Benjamin Franklin. Franklin sent him to America, where his pen soon brought him fame and later fortune.

Though painful, revolutions are great opportunities. A quick look at the list of the world's ten richest people in 2001 shows why:

- **Bill Gates**—Microsoft founder and software revolutionary
- **Warren Buffett**—Value-investing revolutionary and Chairman of Berkshire Hathaway
- **Karl and Theo Albrecht**—Founders of the revolutionary Aldi chain of German discount stores
- **Paul Allen**—Microsoft founder and software revolutionary
- **Larry Ellison**—Oracle Corporation founder and software revolutionary
- **Alice, Helen, Jim, John, and Robson Walton**—Heirs of retailing revolutionary and Wal-Mart founder Sam Walton

In business, revolutions are enormously profitable. Revolutionaries (or their heirs) dominate the list of the world's wealthiest. Some lead the revolution in a new field like Bill Gates, Paul Allen or Larry Ellison. Warren Buffet built his fortune by rebelling against trendy investment strategies, while the Walton and Albrecht fortunes occupy six spots from pursuing the ancient model of discount retailing with revolutionary efficiency. If you are ambitious, it is not a question of whether you should be a revolutionary, but which revolution to lead.

Wanted: Revolutionaries

*If you would not be forgotten as soon as you
are dead, either write things worth reading
or do things worth the writing.*
—BENJAMIN FRANKLIN

People Win Revolutions

It wasn't organizations that prevailed in the American Revolution. Reluctant or enthusiastic, people won the war and founded the American Republic. Some were rich. John Hancock was a wealthy Boston ship owner and merchant who inherited a fortune from a rich uncle. Flamboyant as his famous signature, the revolution was the perfect opportunity for his personal ambitions. Others were motivated upstarts. Alexander Hamilton, a proud orphan from the West Indies, embraced the Revolution to prove his worth and overcome his disreputable origins.

There were men of conscience. John Adams was a family man working to build a comfortable law practice. He fought for justice, even when right was with the enemy. And there were tough, ordinary people like Mary Hayes, who became famous carrying water under fire as Molly Pitcher, enduring squalid army camps and the horrors of battle.

These revolutionaries prevailed with little help from government, or even from most of their neighbors. Patriots were a minority. Most colonists were neutral during the war, or remained loyal to the Crown. Colonial organizations didn't do much for the Revolution either. The

Continental Congress was ineffective, the States jealous and quarrelsome. Government largely gave legitimacy to the heroic efforts of dedicated Patriots. It was revolutionaries, men and women with dreams and convictions, who moved the world a step closer to freedom, equality, and prosperity.

Individuals can make dramatic differences. American-born financier George Peabody pioneered a revolution in urban housing when he endowed the Peabody Donation Fund in 1862. It provided affordable housing for more than twenty thousand of the poor of London. Peabody's farsighted investment has helped many generations break the cycle of poverty and increase the prosperity of their families and nation.

CHAPTER TWO

STARTING YOUR REVOLUTION

Be Passionate

Yet the object is worth rivers of blood,
and years of desolation.

—THOMAS JEFFERSON,
IN A LETTER TO JOHN ADAMS, 1823

Samuel Adams

Revolutions need fervent, heartfelt passion to succeed. In the American Revolution, Samuel Adams personified that passion. Born into a prosperous family, Adams lost everything, a loss he blamed on arrogant royal officials. Embittered toward the British, Adams became fervently committed to American independence.

Adams's passion drove him to organize the Sons of Liberty to resist British taxation. He was so effective that General Gage, the British military governor, offered Adams a lucrative government post if he would stop leading the opposition. Adams had been reduced to poverty, and would remain poor for the rest of his life. But he was passionate about his revolution. He refused the British bribe and continued his brilliant coordination of the rebellion in Boston.

Passion is a revolutionary's most effective tool for overcoming obstacles. Charles Goodyear popularized the use of rubber because it was his passion. Rubber had flopped as a commercial product. It cracked when cold and melted when hot. Goodyear loved rubber anyway. He dedicated his life to fixing its flaws. When he ran out of money, he moved his family into his factory and ate from rubber plates. His children were often hungry, and Goodyear was often in debtor's prison. His commitment was so complete that after years of failure he stumbled across the vulcan reaction process that finally made rubber into a useful product.

Begin

I rejoice that America has resisted. Three million of people, so dead to all the feelings of liberty, as voluntarily to submit to he slaves, would have been fit instruments to make slaves of the rest.

—WILLIAM PITT,
IN A SPEECH IN THE HOUSE OF COMMONS, MARCH 6, 1766

Samuel Adams Orchestrates a Revolution

Samuel Adams knew that the American colonies were not ready for their independence from Britain. Most Americans didn't want independence. Even Patriot leaders were working for a just reconciliation with Britain. Rebelling against the king was unthinkable. But Adams understood that a revolution must begin before opinions could be changed.

To inspire a revolutionary spirit, Adams and his colleagues orchestrated a brilliant campaign of provocation. Stamp Tax officers were intimidated into resigning their posts. American businesses refused to buy the stamps, suspending operations for which stamps were needed or violating the law. Patriots tightened a colonial boycott of British imports until London merchants begged Parliament to repeal the Stamp Act. Parliament finally complied.

With the end of the Stamp Act, colonists realized that they had power. Independence was no longer unthinkable. While most Patriots still wanted reconciliation with Britain, they would now only accept it on their terms. Sam Adams had turned his countrymen into revolutionaries by initiating the rebellion.

Like Adams's rebellion, your revolution must begin before it can change minds. Steve Demos started White Wave, Inc. in 1977 to bring soy products to the American diet. But sales grew slowly because consumers were not familiar with the early forms of soy, such as tofu. Demos had to build an entire culinary, production, and merchandising infrastructure that put soy products in familiar forms like soy milk in dairy case cartons before customers were won over. Today, soy is one of the fastest-growing categories of food products.

It Can Work Now

You may delay, but time will not.

—BENJAMIN FRANKLIN

The Townshend Acts

After the repeal of the Stamp Act, Britain still had a huge revenue shortfall. In desperation, its Chancellor of the Exchequer, Charles Townshend, imposed a series of colonial duties. Americans again resisted. Patriots organized boycotts and threatened customs agents. Resistance was so violent that British officials asked for troops to enforce the collection of duties.

Americans made it clear that any attempt to impose taxes would lead to a rebellion. It was a bold position for the colonists to take. America wasn't ready to fight Britain in a war. They had nothing to fight with, no army, no navy, and no government. But Patriots like Sam Adams couldn't foresee when America would be strong enough to defy British military might. If they waited, Britain might put the colonies more firmly under its control. So Patriots resisted British actions and risked conflict rather than wait for a more opportune time.

It is only human to wait for favorable circumstances. Individuals put off their dreams until they can afford them. Corporations delay innovations for stable financial conditions or clear market directions. But waiting doesn't help. The time is never right for innovative change until it is too late. Revolutionaries forge ahead even in unfavorable circumstances.

The year 1837 wasn't the most auspicious time to start a soap revolution in Cincinnati. There were already fourteen established soap- and candle-making competitors in the area. The economy was in a shambles. Factories and farms were going bankrupt. There were rumors that the whole country was insolvent. It was one of the bleakest recessions in American history. William Procter and James Gamble started a business anyway.

Through hard work, Procter and Gamble survived despite the horrendous economy and fierce competition. When the Civil War threatened to tear the country apart, they turned the conflict into another opportunity. They bought a huge supply of rosin for making soap before the war interrupted supplies. With ample raw materials, they won a large contract to supply the Union army with soap. Boxes with the distinctive Procter & Gamble logo could be found wherever the army went. When soldiers returned home from the war, they all remembered Procter & Gamble. The company was able to expand even faster after the war. There are good times and there are bad times, but the best time for innovation is always now.

Positioning the Revolution

Glass, China, and Reputation, are easily crack'd, and never well mended.

—Benjamin Franklin

The Boston Massacre, 1770

Patriot resistance escalated tensions between colonists and British troops and officials. On March 5, 1770, British troops fired on a Boston mob that was harassing them, killing several. It is unclear who was at fault, although John Adams won the acquittal of the commander of the soldiers. But Samuel Adams seized on the incident to position the rebellion.

Like all revolutions, the most important struggle in the American Revolution was the battle for public opinion. Samuel Adams had to overcome the stigma of treason. No American wanted to be a traitor. So Adams asked Paul Revere to create a print showing British soldiers gunning down peaceful citizens in the Boston Massacre. Revere, a brilliant silversmith and sometime dentist, also produced engravings. His print of the Boston Massacre was his most important contribution to the revolution. By showing the British as heartless oppressors, American rebels became Patriots. The print was widely circulated, galvanizing opposition to the British.

Positive positioning and publicity is essential to innovation. Dale Chihuly has turned his art in to a multimillion-dollar business by perfecting the art of positive positioning. Chihuly creates spectacular glass sculpture. But the core of his success is his unique flair for attracting attention to the beauty he creates. For Chihuly, generating publicity is a full-time task. He employs a cameraman to record everything he does. Every exhibition and installation is meticulously filmed. The footage is used in a blizzard of press releases, documentaries, and books that promote him and his art. Chihuly understands that getting the message out about what he does is as important as the art itself.

Take Action

*When is the time for brave men to exert themselves
in the cause of liberty and their country, if this is not?*

—George Washington,
in a letter to General Philip Schuyler, December 24, 1775

The Boston Tea Party, December 16, 1773

Faced with imminent rebellion in the colonies, the British repealed the Townshend Acts in 1770. Tensions were so high that King George's government left the colonies alone. British forbearance might have let the rebellion burn out, but the British had another colonial problem. The vital East India Company was almost bankrupt. It needed money and had a huge store of tea that it had not sold. The new prime minister, Lord Frederick North, decided to sell the surplus tea to the colonists with only the Townshend duties. Removing all the other taxes, the East India tea was cheaper than smuggled tea. North was certain that Americans couldn't resist the bargain, unintentionally paying taxes and saving the East India Company.

Patriot leaders saw North's bargain as a trick to establish a tax precedent. They were also angry that the lucrative contracts to sell the tea were given to Crown favorites. Throughout the colonies, the Sons of Liberty demanded that the tea not be landed. The merchants who carried the tea had no intention of unloading it after seeing the violent local opposition, but British officials in Boston closed the harbor to prevent the tea ships from leaving.

Samuel Adams saw an opportunity to escalate the rebellion. When British officials refused demands that the tea ships leave, Adams took action. Companies of colonists disguised as Native Americans rowed to the ships and destroyed the tea shipment.

Adams's provocation set off a chain reaction of rebellion and repression. The tea on the *London* was confiscated in Charleston. New York Sons of Liberty, again disguised as Indians, dumped their own load of tea into the harbor. The British sent more troops and closed the port of Boston. Americans responded by preparing to fight, gathering arms and raising militia companies. Colonial leaders called for a Continental Congress to coordinate resistance. War was imminent.

Revolutions start because someone takes action. In 1958, Jack Kilby, a Texas Instruments engineer, conceived of building transistors as a single integrated circuit instead of wiring them together. It would have been easy to ignore the idea. Wiring transistors was simple, cheap, and well-understood. The equipment and procedures to build production-integrated circuits would have to be created from scratch. It would be expensive and take years of investment before making a dime. But TI recognized that the idea had merit, and they acted. So did Robert Noyce at Fairchild Semiconductor. Each began refining the techniques, building the equipment, and developing strategies that made integrated circuits a reality and changed the world.

Like-Minded Revolutionaries

Associate yourself with men of good quality.

—George Washington

Becoming a Revolutionary

Unlike Samuel Adams, most of the leaders of the American Revolution were not natural revolutionaries. When delegates from the various colonies met in the First Continental Congress in September 1774, they declared British reprisals illegal, but also reiterated their desire to remain part of the empire. Patriot leaders needed more exposure to radical ideas before becoming revolutionaries themselves.

John Adams was typical. At the start of the unrest, Adams wanted justice, not a revolution. But Adams joined the Caucus Club, where he came in contact with revolutionary ideas and people. The Caucus Club exposed him to the possibilities of radical changes. As the conflict between America and Britain deepened, he saw the necessity of a drastic change in relations, even independence.

George Washington was a rich planter. He did not want a revolution upsetting the economy. Farming was hard enough without war, upheaval, and anarchy. Then Washington was elected to the Virginia House of Burgesses, where he came in contact with the more radical thinking of George Mason, Patrick Henry and Richard Henry Lee. By 1769, he was a leader of the opposition to the Townshend Acts. He became a revolutionary by associating with rebels.

You too can become a revolutionary by meeting regularly with people who understand the need for innovation. A few months before Michael Dell, the founder of Dell Computer, started selling computers from his college dorm room, he skipped a week of high school to attend the National Computer Conference. There he was able to talk with almost everyone who was involved in the infant personal computer revolution. He learned the problems and the opportunities. He quickly became a revolutionary himself.

Redundancies

But in this world nothing can be said to be certain,
except death and taxes.

—BENJAMIN FRANKLIN,
IN A LETTER TO JEAN-BAPTISTE LEROY, NOVEMBER 13, 1789

Paul Revere's Other Contribution

After the Boston Tea Party, Samuel Adams and John Hancock continued to stir up trouble from nearby Lexington. Patriots drilled in their militias and gathered an arsenal at Concord. The British decided to march from Boston to capture Adams, Hancock, and the Patriots' weapons. It was impossible to keep the plan secret, but no one knew when the attack would take place. The rebels needed time to gather their irregular troops if they were to stop the British. Paul Revere was assigned to give warning of the attack.

Paul Revere was an experienced Patriot messenger. He knew that things could go wrong. And so Revere made certain that his plan for warning the Patriots had redundancies. On April 18, 1775, Paul Revere learned that British troops were ready to move. He hung two lanterns in the bell tower of Christ Church to signal to the Charlestown Sons of Liberty that the British were coming across the harbor. Revere had arranged the signals a week earlier to get the warning out even if the British detained him. Next, Revere sent his coconspirator, William Dawes, to spread the alarm via the land route across the Boston neck. Then Revere slipped out of Boston himself. Two friends rowed him across the bay to Charlestown. He borrowed a horse, checked that his signal had been received, and rode off spreading the alarm.

Dawes and his friend Samuel Prescott joined Revere in Lexington. Together they rode toward Concord where the rebel stores of arms and munitions were kept. On the way, they were surprised by a British patrol. Dawes and Prescott escaped and rode on to spread the alarm, but Revere was captured. He never made it to every Middlesex village and farm. But because of the redundancies in his plan, the minutemen gathered anyway. After a brief skirmish at Lexington, Patriots drove the British regulars all the way from Concord to Charlestown with heavy losses.

Aspiring revolutionaries always need a backup strategy. Innovation is too uncertain to rely on a single plan. William Wrigley Jr. became a chewing gum millionaire as a backup strategy. He was selling soap door-to-door, giving away baking soda to encourage sales. The baking soda was more popular, so he switched to selling it, using chewing gum as his new incentive. The gum proved a huge success and made his fortune.

Improvisation

He that riseth late, must trot all day.

—BENJAMIN FRANKLIN

Ticonderoga, May 10, 1775

New Englanders feared that the British would invade the northern colonies by marching south from Canada along Lake Champlain. Benedict Arnold, an ambitious New Haven apothecary and merchant, formulated a bold plan to seize the British forts on Lake Champlain and hold them against any invasion from Canada. Arnold wrangled a provisional colonel's commission from the Massachusetts Committee of Safety and headed for Lake Champlain while others recruited for his small army. He met up with Ethan Allen and his Green Mountain Boys, who were also planning to take the British forts. Arnold and Allen fought over command, but realized the issue was less important than surprising the British garrisons. Rather than organize, they marched for Lake Champlain.

At the lake, the Patriots found only enough boats to carry eighty men across to Fort Ticonderoga. Again, they improvised and crossed immediately. Their small detachment surprised and easily captured the garrison. Patriots took His Majesty's Fort at Crown Point the next day. Some of Arnold's own recruits arrived, and he sailed with them to St. Johns, where he captured the small garrison and an armed sloop. Arnold renamed the sloop *Enterprise,* the first of a series of American warships to bear the name. He then withdrew to Ticonderoga to organize a defense against a British counterattack.

The Patriots improvised to gain control of Lake Champlain. They acted long before a more organized effort could be launched, and before the British could reinforce their vulnerable outposts.

When there is an opportunity, revolutionaries act, even if they must improvise. When Sandra Kurtzig started ASK Computer Systems, she had no computer for developing software. She and her programmers borrowed computer time from a HP facility at night to write the code for one of the first inventory management systems. Kurtzig's early improvisation gave her product an invaluable head start in the market.

Ask for the Job

Fear not death; for the sooner we die,
the longer shall we be immortal.

—BENJAMIN FRANKLIN

Congress Appoints Washington Commander in Chief

When the Second Continental Congress met to discuss the rebellion in Massachusetts, George Washington attended in uniform. As the only delegate in uniform, Washington was volunteering for the job of commander in chief of the Continental Army. He had been one of the most influential leaders of the First Continental Congress. Now, delegates were reminded that, twenty years earlier, Washington's cool bravery had saved the British army from complete annihilation during the French and Indian War.

Washington always denied that he desired command, but there is no question that he wished to lead the rebellion. By wearing his uniform, he made certain that everyone knew he wanted the appointment and was aware of his qualifications. Otherwise, command might have gone to Artemas Ward or John Hancock. Ward, a native New Englander, was already head of the army around Boston. Hancock had no military experience, but his ego was huge. As president of the Continental Congress, he had the political influence to win the appointment.

Unfortunately for Hancock, John Adams and others realized that the revolution would be strengthened if a Virginian were given command. The rebellion was still largely confined to New England. Selecting a southern commander in chief would symbolically spread the revolution to the southern colonies. Washington was the obvious choice.

In Congress, Adams rose to nominate a commander. Hancock prepared himself to accept the assignment. Instead, Adams nominated Washington. A strange debate ensued, with southerners supporting Ward to reduce their involvement and New Englanders pushing for Washington to draw in the south. New England won. The next day, George Washington was named the commander in chief of the newly authorized Continental Army.

Revolutionaries ask for jobs, even if they do not exist. As a student, Ian Ballantine found a loophole in American copyright laws that allowed British paperback books to be imported cheaply. He used the loophole to get his first job, shipping British paperbacks to the United States for Penguin Books. He expanded on the idea to start Bantam Books, this time selling paperbacks by American authors. And he gave himself one more job, founding Ballantine Books to simultaneously release hardcover and paperback books in different channels. Asking for one job that hadn't existed led to a publishing empire.

Never Underestimate the Competition

Don't fire until you see the whites of their eyes.

—William Prescott,
Patriot officer, to his men at Breeds Hill

Bunker Hill, June 17, 1775

The Patriots occupied Breeds Hill above Charlestown to give their artillery command of Boston Harbor. The British had to expel the rebels or be cut off from resupply by sea. General Thomas Gage ordered British general William Howe to take the Patriot positions. Howe had arrived in May with Henry Clinton and John Burgoyne to support Gage, whom Howe would soon replace. Howe was an experienced officer and sympathetic to the American cause, but could never bring himself to energetically pursue and defeat the rebels. He had little respect for Patriot fighting skills. He disdained the guerilla tactics of the rebels at Lexington and Concord as cowardly. And so Howe's expedition to dislodge the Americans badly underestimated their capabilities.

The Patriots should have been wiped out. They were isolated on a peninsula and could have been easily flanked and cut off. Howe didn't bother. British warships should have pounded the Patriot fortifications before an attack. Howe didn't wait. His men marched straight at

Patriot lines and were slaughtered. Horrified, the British regrouped and attacked again. They were repulsed once more with frightening losses. Unwilling to be beaten by a smaller force of farmers and tradesmen, the British reformed their lines and attacked once again. By now, the Patriots were almost out of powder. Confused, Patriot reserves on the mainland failed to reinforce the Breeds Hill position or bring more powder. Patriot defenders had to give way before the British attack. The British finally took the hill, but at a terrible price.

It is foolish to underestimate the competition. Schlitz Beer was a strong national brand when the company decided its rivals would let it get away with cheapening its product. Corn syrup was substituted for barley, the fermentation time was sharply cut, and foaming chemicals were added. But its competitors pounced on this newer, less tasty brew, and vigorously seized market share. The Schlitz brand was all but destroyed and the company was sold to Strohs in 1982.

The Folly of Pride

So contemptible is the rebel force now in all parts…so vast is our superiority that no resistance on their part can obstruct a speedy suppression of the rebellion.

—Lord George Germain,
British Colonial Secretary

The Colonies Sue for Peace, July 1775

In 1775, Thomas Jefferson drafted his first declaration for the Continental Congress, *A Declaration by the Representatives of the United Colonies of North-America, Now Met in Congress at Philadelphia Setting Forth the Causes and Necessity of Their Taking Up Arms*. It was sent to King George with the *Olive Branch Petition*. The documents explained that the colonies didn't necessarily want independence but were unwilling to be enslaved. Jefferson's first draft was considered too harsh, so another delegate, John Dickinson, wrote a second, more conciliatory draft. Congress was careful to not be misunderstood. Even as they raised money and arms to fight the British, the Continental Congress made a last attempt at reconciliation.

The British should have taken the offer. It was a bargain compared to the cost of the next eight years of war. But the King found the offer insulting. He was too proud to deal with traitors. Britain refused the offer and the price of peace went up. A year later, Americans would only accept independence.

> Don't let pride keep you from a solution. Thomas Edison developed an all-concrete house that could be cheaply cast on site. The three-story, six-room houses were much less expensive than conventional houses to construct, but they were ugly. Edison had correctly anticipated the mass production construction strategies that would be popular after World War II. But he was so enamored of his idea that he refused to allow changes to his design so that the homes would sell. Edison was finally forced to abandon the project.

Revolutions Organize

*Never exceed your rights, and they will
soon become unlimited.*

—JEAN JACQUES ROUSSEAU

Washington Takes Command, July 3, 1775

Washington took command of the Patriot forces around Boston. His army didn't have enough ammunition for more than a skirmish. The fiercely independent militiamen hated military regimentation as much as British taxes. Soldiers came and went as they pleased, even abandoning duty on the army's defensive line if they had more pressing business. When there was no fighting, they wanted to return to their farms and shops. They had no use for drills and organization. And their officers were unskilled at enforcing orders.

Washington understood that while ad hoc efforts might start revolutions, they needed organization to win it. He began by asserting his authority. He cracked down on his officers who were ignoring orders, petitioning for alternate plans, or communicating with the British on their own initiative. He demanded discipline and limited the furloughs that often left units unable to carry out assignments. And he found powder and guns. Through tireless work, he forged the mob of enthusiastic men into a real army.

All revolutions must eventually organize on an appropriate scale to win. Kiichiro Toyoda developed a car and a truck for his family's Toyoda Automatic Loom Works. But volumes were too small to compete with foreign imports. Toyoda calculated that he needed to build 1,500 units annually. Plant and equipment costs would total six times the capitalization of the parent company. Toyoda did not hesitate, raising the capital and organizing the Toyota Motor Corporation to take advantage the revolutionary opportunity to build automobiles in Japan.

CHAPTER THREE

THE STRUGGLE

Be Bold

Well done is better than well said.

—BENJAMIN FRANKLIN

The Invasion of Canada, 1775

The American invasion of Canada was unusually bold. British troops still occupied Boston. The Continental Congress was trying to negotiate its way back into the British Empire. And the raw American troops would have to fight far from home. But Patriots feared that the British would recruit an army in Canada and invade south along Lake Champlain, cutting off New England from the rest of the colonies. Canada was weakly defended but was certain to be reinforced in the next year. If the Patriots could take Canada and win over the local population to their cause, it would seriously weaken the British position.

In late 1775, the Continental Congress ordered two American armies under General Richard Montgomery and Colonel Benedict Arnold into Canada. Montgomery traveled north along Lake Champlain. He took

Montreal and sent Royal Governor Guy Carleton and his small force down the Saint Lawrence River toward Quebec City. If the Patriots could take the fortress of Quebec City, Canada would be in rebel hands. The bold invasion had almost succeeded.

Caution does not win revolutions. Critics questioned Philip Anschutz's purchase of the Denver & Rio Grande Western Railroad for $500 million in 1984. Railroads were not attractive investments then, but Anschutz's bold move paid for itself twice over. He leveraged ownership of the railroad to acquire the Southern Pacific Railroad. One of his companies, Qwest, then bought the rights to lay fiber on railroad right-of-ways before he sold the railroads to Union Pacific Railroad for $3.9 billion. Qwest leveraged its fiber network to buy baby bell US West. Boldly bucking the odds can pay off handsomely.

Plan Like a Pessimist

There is nothing so delusive as prosperity.

—Richard Henry Lee,
to Samuel Adams in a July 27, 1777 letter

From Maine to Quebec

Benedict Arnold led his invasion force through the wilderness from Maine to Quebec City. Few Americans had ever used the rugged route. But if it worked, the Patriots could surprise Quebec City before it could be adequately defended. The opportunity was so promising that the expedition was organized.

Patriot plans turned out to be wildly optimistic. The route was twice as long as anyone anticipated, and far more rugged. Worse, torrential rains flooded the area, making travel by land or river impossible. The army lost many of its supplies, and deserters carried off the rest. It was remarkable that so many of the soldiers completed the march. They arrived at Quebec exhausted, ragged, and starving a few days after Governor Carleton and his small army reached the city from Montreal. Too late to take the city by surprise, Arnold's army laid siege to the fortress city and were soon joined by Montgomery and his army.

Revolutionaries must be optimists. However, because revolutions never develop according to plan, even the most optimistic innovators must learn to plan like pessimists if they are to prevail. Like most human enterprises, little in the American Revolution occurred as expected. Torrential rains, floods, a lack of boats, too much ice, too little ice, wet powder, fog, no fog, miscommunication, and stupidity all turned good plans into fiascoes. And the more optimistic the Patriot plans were, the more likely they were to fail.

Ill luck will threaten your revolution unless you anticipate the unexpected. Elisha Otis was an optimist. He was headed for the California gold fields after he finished a job building a hoist for a bedstead factory in Yonkers. But he preserved enough pessimism to add a ratchet mechanism to the hoist to prevent it from falling if its rope broke. His customer loved it. So did hundreds of others who appreciated just how uncertain life can be. Otis became rich installing elevators that wouldn't drop even when things went wrong.

Don't Alienate Potential Allies

Be slow in chusing a friend, slower in changing.

—BENJAMIN FRANKLIN

Patriots and Loyalists Make Enemies

The Continental Congress shot itself in the foot in 1775. It published a document listing Roman Catholics as potential dangers to American freedom. Quebec's royal governor, Guy Carleton, was quick to take advantage of the document to blunt the Patriot invasion of Canada. Carleton was an energetic and resourceful leader. The American Revolution might have ended differently if he had been governor of Massachusetts instead of Quebec. Carleton used the American document to convince his French-Catholic subjects that they were better off remaining loyal to the British than supporting the American rebels. The ill-conceived document seriously damaged Patriot efforts to recruit French Canadians to join their invasion of Canada. As the war progressed, Catholics and Catholic countries were the Revolution's best allies. Congress allowed its personal prejudices to get in the way of sound policy.

Fortunately, the British were equally adept at alienating potential allies. The governor of Virginia, John Murray, tried to crush the rebellion by raising an army of slaves emancipated from their rebellious masters. A slave rebellion was so feared in Virginia that Murray immediately galvanized opposition to British rule in the colony. Murray was driven from Virginia, which remained a rebel stronghold for the rest of the war.

Revolutionaries like to make bold claims. They are, after all, leading a revolution. But because you never know where a revolution will go, scrutinize all communication to avoid alienating potential allies. Department store chain Neiman Marcus sent thank-you letters to customers who had purchased expensive gifts. Unfortunately, many of the wives who opened of these letters would not be the recipients of the gifts. Neiman Marcus failed to consider secondary audiences, which earned them the wrath of philandering but otherwise big-spending customers.

Expect to Win

Liberty, when it begins to take root,
is a plant of rapid growth.

—GEORGE WASHINGTON

The Assault on Quebec, January 1, 1775

The Patriot army in Canada was too weak and too far from home to hold the colony without local support. French Canadians had no great loyalty to the British, but wanted to join the winning side. It didn't look like it would be the Americans. The Patriot army was ragged, starving, and sick. The Americans needed a decisive victory to convince Canadians to join the rebellion. They had to take Quebec City and defeat Governor Carleton before British reinforcements arrived in the spring if they were to win Canadian support and hold Canada.

But Quebec City was virtually impregnable. With stout, cannon-studded walls, it was the most formidable fortress on the continent. Most Patriots despaired of success. Hungry, homesick, and cold, they planned to march for home when their enlistments were up at the end of the year.

Montgomery and Arnold didn't share the pessimism of their men. They decided to attempt a last attack on the city before their army disbanded. They launched a two-pronged surprise attack before dawn during a blinding snowstorm. The assault almost worked. Colonel Arnold was wounded, but Captain Daniel Morgan continued the attack with Arnold's column. Morgan was a fearless fighter with a deep hatred of the British. Years earlier, he had decked a haughty British lieutenant who struck him with his sword. The British gave Morgan 499 lashes. Now he could take his revenge.

Morgan breached the first barricade and raced into the lower city. The defenders melted away in panic. The Patriots were poised to rout the British from inside the city. But when Morgan urged his men forward, they refused to move. It seemed too incredible for victory to be within their grasp. Fearful of defeat, Morgan's men refused to advance until Montgomery's force joined them.

Montgomery's column was not coming. Montgomery had been killed when the assault started. Although resistance was otherwise light, his men expected to fail and ran at this first setback. While Morgan's column waited for the reinforcements that would never come, the initiative passed to the British. The defenders rallied, cut off the Patriots in the city, and captured much of their army. The American invasion of Canada was over.

It might have been different if Morgan's or Montgomery's columns had pressed forward. The surprise attack could have worked if Patriot soldiers hadn't expected it to fail.

Revolutionaries must expect to succeed. In 1916, David Sarnoff had an idea for a radio music box. There wasn't much interest in the concept at his employer, Marconi. The major profits in radio came from international and maritime communications. Sarnoff pushed for his idea again when Marconi became RCA. However, executives still felt that radio receivers were too expensive and crude for broadcasts to homes. Expecting failure, they waited to act. But radio was ready to succeed. A Westinghouse engineer began broadcasting from his garage, attracting a dedicated following of local radio hobbyists. Westinghouse started its own broadcasts. Department stores sold every crude, expensive radio on their shelves. The radio revolution was in full swing, far ahead of expectations.

Avoid Diversions

*Never buy what you do not want, because it is cheap;
it will be dear to you.*

—THOMAS JEFFERSON

The End of the Canadian Campaign, 1776

The remnant of the Patriot army in Canada retreated from Quebec City to Montreal. Governor Carleton was reinforced from Britain and pursued the ragged Patriots. Carleton retook Montreal, then moved south to invade the American colonies. Benedict Arnold hastily gathered a fleet on Lake Champlain to block the British. Carleton was forced to assemble his own fleet, including several ships that were dragged to the lake. The inferior American fleet made a spirited defense but was destroyed after two days of fighting. Still, the fleet had done its job. It was almost winter, forcing Carleton to abandon his invasion.

The invasion of Canada was costly, but Patriots learned from the mistake. They understood that Canada was no longer a strategic objective. Although the British would use Canada for a future invasion, it was easier to defend against attacks on American soil. Congress considered another invasion in 1777, but abandoned the idea. Canada was a diversion that could be ignored.

Ignore the diversions to your innovation. While you will be tempted to pursue all of your innovation's opportunities, focusing your strategies and resources will be far more effective.

Nokia Corporation was created from the merger of forestry, rubber, and cable companies in 1967. Years later, it got into mobile phones in keeping with its diverse nature. The mobile phone group lost money, but the unit's head, Jorma Ollila, saw its potential. When Ollila was named CEO of Nokia, he sold off the other distractions and dedicated Nokia to producing great mobile phones. With all the energy of the company focused behind winning with one product, Nokia made rapid progress. It passed market leader Motorola in just a few years. Nokia would have never dominated cellular telephones if it had been worrying about paper products, rubber boots, and televisions at the same time.

Recognize Your Strengths

The battle, sir, is not to the strong alone;
it is to the vigilant, the active, the brave.

—PATRICK HENRY,
IN A SPEECH AT THE VIRGINIA CONVENTION

The Liberation of Boston, 1776

George Washington knew his amateur soldiers lacked the skill to storm the British fortifications guarding Boston. Instead, he created a strategy that took advantage of his army's natural strengths. He planned to place his artillery on Dorchester Heights, where it could bombard the city and British fleet. The British left the strategic heights unoccupied because they believed that they could destroy any Patriot battery before it became operational. But Washington understood that while his army couldn't march or use bayonets, they were unmatched at battlefield engineering. American soldiers could dig, cart, and build better than any army in the world. Washington planned to use those skills to erect fortifications for his artillery on Dorchester Heights before the British could react.

Washington sent Henry Knox to collect the cannon captured at Fort Ticonderoga. Knox moved scores of massive artillery pieces three hundred miles back to Boston over mountain trails in the middle of winter. With cannon in hand, Washington executed the second half of his plan. His men made careful preparations to occupy Dorchester Heights and erect instant fortifications. The frozen ground prevented the digging of trenches. Instead, Patriots prepared frames that could be packed with hay and barrels of rock and earth that could be wheeled into place.

Washington made his move in early March. At dark, Patriot soldiers secured Dorchester Heights. Behind them came more men and hundreds of carts of material for the fortifications. Within hours, they had erected two forts. When dawn finally revealed the Patriots' labors, the British were astonished. Defensive works had appeared overnight, as if by magic. General Howe, in command after Gage's recall, made feeble preparations to attack the American position but ultimately admitted defeat. He loaded his army and Loyalist supporters on transports and sailed for Halifax. The Patriots had liberated Boston.

> Revolutionaries must use their native advantages to win. The airline business is tough to break into. It relies heavily on expensive fixed assets, planes, and gates. Most new entrants, and many established airlines, don't make it. Southwest Airlines has been an exception because it has relied on its own unique strengths.
>
> Southwest started service flying between convenient downtown airports after Dallas and Houston built large new airports far from city centers. Business travelers saved valuable time traveling to and from the nearby business districts. Southwest improved on this advantage with frequent flights and brief stops at the gate. Competitors couldn't match it for rapid trips between Texas cities. But the efficiencies Southwest developed also enabled it to move beyond its downtown airport strategy. With the highest productivity in the industry, Southwest is cheaper to fly and more profitable than many of the major carriers. As of January 2002, Southwest has had an astounding string of 29 profitable years.

Credit Where Credit is Due

*Advertisements contain the only truths to be
relied on in a newspaper.*

—THOMAS JEFFERSON,
IN A LETTER, 1819

Charleston, June 28, 1776

Americans learned that the British under General Clinton planned to capture Charleston to gain control of the southern colonies. Patriots prepared feverishly to defend the city. Colonel William Moultrie constructed a fort on Sullivan's Island at the entrance to Charleston Harbor to protect the city from a naval attack. There wasn't time to build a proper fortress, so Moultrie improvised. He constructed parallel walls of palmetto logs and filled the space in between with earth. It was an unlikely looking fort, but it was solidly built.

The Continental Congress sent General Charles Lee to oversee the defense of Charleston. Lee was a coarse soldier of fortune. He had served the in American colonies, Canada, Portugal, and Poland and had a high opinion of his own abilities. Lee arrived just before the fighting commenced. He lost no time in telling the locals that everything they had done was wrong. He was particularly critical of Moultrie's palmetto fort. Claiming that it "could not hold out half an hour," he tried to have the fort abandoned. When the locals refused (this was a very democratic army), Lee withdrew critical troops and powder from Moultrie's fort.

After several false starts, the British attack came straight at Moultrie's palmetto fortress. The fleet anchored off Sullivan's Island and began a massive bombardment. But the walls of the fort held while Moultrie's cannon devastated the British ships. Moultrie ran low on powder and appealed to Lee for more. Lee responded by ordering Moultrie to retreat. Moultrie held his ground against Lee and the British and continued to fight. He had to stop firing for hours at a time because of lack of powder. But he was still able to maul the British, who could not withdraw while the wind and tide were against them. The Patriots won a great victory at Charleston, and it would have been a decisive victory except for Lee.

After the battle, General Lee returned north. As the commander at Charleston, Congress rewarded him with splendid bonus for his triumph, even though he had nothing to do with the victory. His reputation and his ego now far exceeded his abilities as a commander, allowing him to do much harm to the revolution.

It pays to give credit only where it is due. Gil Amelio became CEO of Apple Computer, Inc. because of his reputation for turning around National Semiconductor. Amelio took over at National during one of the semiconductor industry's slumps. Chip prices regularly rise and fall as demand exceeds or lags behind capacity. After Amelio became CEO, semiconductor demand exceeded supply and National rode the industry-wide price increases to profitability. National's recovery won Amelio the top post at Apple. But at Apple there was no external trend to bail him out. He quickly floundered and was forced out in 1997.

The Energy of Opportunity

Money is the seed of money,
and the first guinea is sometimes more difficult
to acquire than the second million.

—Jean Jacques Rousseau

Upward Mobility in America

In eighteenth-century Britain, wealthy landowners were forcing country folk off common lands and evicting tenant farmers to convert land to the more lucrative raising of sheep. These uprooted villagers had few choices except the brutal factories of the industrial revolution, crime, or selling themselves as laborers in the colonies. Criminals had even fewer choices. They were hung or transported to the colonies.

Transportation to America was almost a death sentence. Many died of hunger and disease on the long voyage. But in America, these once-desperate people were able to create good lives for themselves. If they survived the period of indentured servitude that paid for their passage, they found that jobs were plentiful and wages good. A growing country and frequent deaths created numerous opportunities. Pickpockets became landowners even though land in Europe was unobtainable for them at almost any price. Former prostitutes married well and became pillars of respectability. The energy that was unleashed by the opportunity of America propelled the colonies into a state of unprecedented growth.

Matthew Lyon was a good example of this. Arriving from Ireland as a destitute boy of fourteen, he worked off his debt and fought in the Revolution. Alongside thousands of indentured Germans, British deserters and desperate younger men, Lyon was energized by the possibility of achieving more than he had ever dreamed was possible. Through hard work, he eventually acquired land, a sawmill, a paper mill, a nail factory, a shipyard, a printing press, and was elected to Congress. His prosperous life was a sharp contrast to the dismal prospects of friends who remained at home.

Grand possibilities are unbeatable motivators. Richard Branson conceived of publishing his own magazine, *Student,* to complain about some of the more unpleasant aspects of school life. Realizing it could be something much grander, Branson threw himself into the project, cold calling major corporations to sell advertising and asking celebrities for interviews and articles. The opportunity was so inspiring that he worked longer and harder than any of his classmates in or out of school. *Student* became the first of Branson's innovative successes, which later included Virgin Atlantic Airways, Virgin Music, Virgin Cola, and the other ventures of the Virgin Group.

CHAPTER FOUR

ORGANIZING THE REVOLUTION

A Motivating Vision

If a man could have half his wishes,
he would double his troubles.

—Benjamin Franklin

Common Sense

In 1776, despite the war, Americans still hoped for reconciliation with Britain. Few wanted independence. Even George Washington and his officers drank a loyal toast to King George each evening. The British government was preparing to take advantage of colonial sentiment with a generous offer for peace that many Americans would have welcomed. But then Thomas Paine sharply altered colonial opinion with his pamphlet *Common Sense*.

Published in early 1776, Paine's pamphlet was a persuasive argument for American independence, and it resonated with the colonists.

An astounding five hundred thousand copies were sold the first year. *Common Sense* blasted the rights of kings to rule. Paine was adamant that the colonies could thrive without Britain and proposed how America could win the war.

The effect of Paine's vision was electrifying. By spring there was much support for American independence. Virginia's convention voted to instruct their delegates to Congress to propose that the colonies formally declare their independence. On June 7, Richard Henry Lee moved that Congress declare the United Colonies to be free and independent, and that they form a Confederation. Thomas Jefferson, John Adams, Benjamin Franklin, Robert R. Livingston, and Roger Sherman were appointed to draft the resolution. Motivated by Paine's vision, the creation of the United States had begun.

> People get excited about grand visions. Jill Conner Browne writes *The Sweet Potato Queens* books, telling her loyal fans that they should be treated like royalty. The idea is so compelling that devotees do more than just buy books for $12.95. They travel from all over the country to Sweet Potato Queen conventions, dress in outrageous costumes and march in parades. Grand visions motivate in ways that the most sophisticated argument is unable to match.

Concise Communication

The most valuable of all talents is that of never using two words when one will do.

— THOMAS JEFFERSON

The Declaration of Independence

Thomas Jefferson was given the task of crafting the Declaration of Independence. After the embarrassment of Congress asking John Dickinson to revise his earlier *Declaration by the Representatives of the United Colonies of North-America, Now Met in Congress at Philadelphia, Setting Forth the Causes and Necessity of Taking Up Arms*, Jefferson was careful to avoid controversy. He used the language and logic of George Mason's Virginia Declaration of Rights to state well-accepted ideas, his words succinctly expressing the principles for which the Revolution was being fought:

> We hold these truths to be self-evident, that all men are created equal, that they are endowed by their Creator with certain unalienable Rights, that among these are Life, Liberty and the pursuit of Happiness—That to secure these rights, Governments are instituted among Men, deriving their just powers from the consent of the governed—That whenever any Form of Government becomes destructive of these ends, it is the Right of the People to alter or to abolish it, and to institute new Government, laying its foundation on such principles and organizing its powers in such form, as to them shall seem most likely to effect their Safety and Happiness.

Then Jefferson listed the grievances the colonies held against their king and concluded they were now independent states. Short and succinct, it is one of the most powerful documents in history.

Good ideas are succinct. Rollin King concisely diagrammed the business plan for Southwest Airlines to Herb Kelleher on a cocktail napkin. The two later cofounded the airline. Although much planning, hard work, and innovation was still required to make the airline a success, a simple, elegant idea was at its core.

Persistence

Little strokes, Fell great oaks.

—BENJAMIN FRANKLIN,
Poor Richard's Almanack 1757

Agreeing for Independence

As Jefferson prepared the draft of the Declaration of Independence, John Adams maneuvered to get Congress to approve it. Adams knew that the vote for independence had to be unanimous. Americans were still hesitant about breaking with Britain. The opposition of any colony would stall the independence movement, and possibly end the rebellion.

On July 1, 1776, Congress considered Richard Henry Lee's motion for independence. Pennsylvania Patriot John Dickinson argued eloquently that separation was premature. John Adams followed with a brilliant speech in favor of independence. But when a preliminary vote was taken afterward, Adams had the votes of only nine delegations.

The Delaware delegation was evenly split, but one pro-independence delegate, Caesar Rodney, was absent caring for his sick wife. Four of seven Pennsylvania delegates were opposed to independence. The New York delegation did not have instructions on how to vote or the freedom to vote their conscience. And South Carolina refused to vote for independence.

Adams was undeterred. He persisted until he found a way to win. After much arm-twisting, South Carolina agreed to support independence if Delaware and Pennsylvania voted for it. The Delaware vote was relatively easy. A messenger was dispatched to convince Caesar Rodney to leave his sick wife to break the tie of his delegation. The Pennsylvania vote took more maneuvering. Two of Pennsylvania's delegates, John Dickinson and Robert Morris, were persuaded to withdraw, giving the pro-independence faction a temporary 3–2 majority.

When Caesar Rodney finally entered the hall on July 2, exhausted, soaked, and muddy after riding through the night, Adams's maneuvering was complete. The Delaware tie was broken and the Delaware delegation voted for independence, followed by South Carolina and Pennsylvania. New York abstained. Independence passed, 12–0, technically unanimous. On July 19, instructions from the New York assembly made it unanimous. Adams's persistence had won the day.

> Persistence pays off. The Haloid Corporation acquired its first photocopying technology in 1935. The need for photocopying was great, but early technology was too primitive to be successful. Haloid didn't give up. In 1947, it bought a new dry copy technology that it rolled out two years later. This product was a modest success. Haloid persisted, investing more in photocopying. Finally, in 1955, Haloid launched the Copyflo copier twenty years after entering the photocopying business. Copyflo was a huge success. Within a few years, the company changed its name to the process that made Copyflo famous, Xerox. Xerox became one of the most successful companies of the 1960s and 1970s because it persisted until it had a winner.

Native Advantages

What you seem to be, be really.

—BENJAMIN FRANKLIN

The Perfect Benjamin Franklin

John Adams's chief ally in guiding the Continental Congress to declare independence was Benjamin Franklin. Unlike Adams, Franklin didn't make rousing speeches. He hated public speaking. But he found witty conversation, dinner, and a glass of Madeira perfect tools to help delegates understand why they shouldn't stand in the way of independence. Franklin's style of persuasion proved just as effective as brilliant oratory.

Franklin hadn't always been satisfied with his own style. As a young man he decided he could achieve perfection. He identified thirteen virtues: temperance, silence, order, resolution, frugality, industry, sincerity, justice, moderation, tranquillity, cleanliness, chastity, and humility. Every week he would work on one, recording the results in a small book. But in the end, he did not change much. He perfected his natural habits of silence and cleanliness, but fell short in other areas such as moderation and frugality, sometimes far short. As he got older and wiser, he abandoned his quest for perfection and relied on his own peculiar strengths: wit, curiosity, and a most congenial manner.

Your natural strengths can bring you success. When assigned to write a business paper for their M.B.A. program, Philip Knight's classmates chose fashionable topics like computers and petroleum refining. Knight understood running, so he wrote his paper on making athletic shoes in the Far East. He knew from many painful blisters that the world could use a better running shoe. After graduation, Knight traveled to Japan, where he agreed to distribute shoes for the Onitsuka Company. Onitsuka also began employing the lightweight designs of Knight's partner, Bill Bowerman. By pursuing their own strengths, Knight, Bowerman, and Nike have done very well.

Disagree and Commit

The discontented Man finds no easy Chair.

—BENJAMIN FRANKLIN

John Dickinson

One prominent member of Congress who did not agree with the Declaration of Independence was John Dickinson. Although he had been a leader in resisting the usurpation of colonial rights, Dickinson thought that Americans would be better off under the unwritten British Constitution than any other government. He believed that independence was a dangerous mistake. Nevertheless, Dickinson recognized that the Declaration of Independence was now a fact and continued to support the Patriot cause. He left Congress to lead Philadelphia's First Battalion of Associators against the British. He was later instrumental in creating both the Articles of Confederation and the Constitution.

Sometimes good revolutionaries must make the best of circumstances they disagree with. AT&T fought for years to maintain its telephony monopoly in the United States. In 1982, it acknowledged that change was inevitable and negotiated its own breakup. While the part of the company that retained the AT&T name has often struggled, shareholders reaped a windfall. The value of Ma Bell's many offshoot companies has appreciated dramatically.

Compelling Value

Wealth is not his that has it, but his that enjoys it.

—Benjamin Franklin

Precedents for Revolution

When the Declaration of Independence was announced, there wasn't enough support among Americans to win a war for independence, but the Founders were confident that support would grow. They pledged "our Lives, our Fortunes and our sacred Honor" because the revolution was built on values their countrymen were committed to: freedom and prosperity.

In the previous century, England had deposed two kings in disputes over taxation. Charles I had tried to impose taxes without the consent of Parliament. Englishmen took up arms against the king in 1642 to preserve their rights. Charles was defeated and beheaded. In 1688, they again deposed another grasping king, James II, this time without bloodshed.

The English passion for freedom was only strengthened in America. Immigrants had to be naturally rebellious to flee Europe for the perils of the new world. Colonists came to prize their freedom and the prosperity they created for themselves. Although most began the revolution as loyal subjects of the king, they ultimately switched their allegiance to enhance their freedom and prosperity.

Compelling values are still a good bet. Greek entrepreneur Stelios Haji-Ioannou has made hundreds of millions in mature, competitive industries by providing more freedom and prosperity through convenient, inexpensive service. His Europe-based easyJet airline and easyRentacar are not saving the world from tyranny, but his customers appreciate the benefits enough to switch allegiances.

The Right Place

The golden age was never the present age.

—BENJAMIN FRANKLIN

Benjamin Franklin's Philadelphia

During the time of the Declaration of Independence, Philadelphia was one of the world's most livable cities. Dark, narrow streets of foul, deep mud were the rule in most other places. The streets of Philadelphia were broad, paved and even lighted by oil lamps at night. With its growing commerce and collection of excellent civic organizations, it was a remarkable place.

Much of Philadelphia's charm came from Benjamin Franklin's genius for improvement. He enthusiastically organized fire companies, a police force, a lending library, a university, a hospital, an insurance company, and many other schemes for civic improvement. Franklin was always grateful to Philadelphia. As a boy, he learned to love printing, but couldn't stand working for his brother or writing for conservative Bostonians. He fled both for Philadelphia. He worked as a printer for a time, and then went to London to find the equipment to start his own printing business. Instead, he found a little too much freedom and had a wild time learning of all the follies he would eventually warn against in his famous *Poor Richard's Almanack*. Franklin finally realized he was not progressing in his career, returned to Philadelphia, and started a printing business.

Printing in Philadelphia was perfect for Franklin. His irreverent wit and progressive thinking were appreciated. Without Boston's opportunities for rebellion or London's temptations, Franklin thrived. Publishing was the perfect outlet for his energies. Franklin wrote his famous almanac and *The Pennsylvania Gazette* and made contacts with leading Pennsylvanians that won him lucrative government contracts.

You must also find the opportunities that bring out your best. Rose Totino made great pizza. The skill seemed of dubious value in Minneapolis during the Depression, but pizza was the right place for her. She took her banker a pizza so he would know what it was and, securing a small loan, opened a restaurant. The restaurant thrived, and Rose and her husband Jim expanded into marketing Totino's pizzas through supermarkets before finally selling the business to Pillsbury.

CHAPTER FIVE

REVOLUTIONARY LEADERSHIP

✶ ✶ ✶

Challenge Your Organization

When men are employed, they are best contented.

—BENJAMIN FRANKLIN

The Continental Army Marches to New York

Washington moved his army to New York in 1776 after the British abandoned Boston. Both sides recognized New York as the strategic center of the war. Whoever controlled New York and the Hudson Valley could unite or divide the colonies. The Continental Army had to control New York if it was to drive the British out and win a military victory.

The move to New York was difficult. The long march strained the organizational and financial resources of the new army. But it arrived in New York stronger than it had ever been around Boston. The army disintegrated in camp. Soldiers became bored. They hated the meaningless tasks created to keep them busy, and either deserted, made trouble, or got sick. Disease and desertion claimed far more soldiers than the British whenever the army stopped moving. Throughout the war, the Continental Army always functioned more efficiently when it was challenged and on the move.

Organizations must be challenged to remain healthy. Xerox's copy machine business was so successful that it grew fatally complacent. It didn't rise to the challenge of smaller competitors, allowing those companies to capture the small copier market and develop superior, low-cost technologies that ultimately destroyed Xerox's once unassailable competitive position.

Recovering from Disaster

After crosses and losses,
men grow humbler and wiser.

—BENJAMIN FRANKLIN

Long Island, 1776

On July 2, 1776, as Congress voted to declare independence, British warships and transports began arriving in New York Harbor. The harbor was soon crowded with almost two hundred ships. Thirty-two thousand well-trained, well-equipped soldiers disembarked and camped on Staten Island. Mountains of supplies, cannon, ammunition, and arms were unloaded. Opposing them, Washington had only eighteen thousand healthy men, the largest Patriot army of the war but still greatly outnumbered. The Patriots were dug in at the southern tip of Manhattan, on the Brooklyn Heights overlooking New York City, and in two fortifications, Fort Washington and Fort Lee on the Hudson River. But the British could use their superior naval transport to isolate and attack these positions at will.

On August 22, the British began their offensive, landing a powerful force on Long Island. In a textbook-perfect operation, General Howe attacked the Continental Army units on the Brooklyn Heights. The Americans fought bravely, but superior British organization quickly found a way to flank the rebel army. Old Jamaica Road had been left unguarded. The British marched into the rear of the Patriot army. Two thousand Patriots on Long Island were killed or captured. The remaining seven thousand were in imminent danger of being overrun. It was a devastating defeat.

Washington reacted to the disaster with incredible calm. He deceived the British with extensive defense preparations and two thousand reinforcements while secretly organizing a withdrawal from Brooklyn to Manhattan. A fleet of small boats gathered at the foot of Brooklyn Heights on August 29. Personally supervising the entire operation, Washington skillfully pulled units from the front line and marched them to the waiting boats. The army slipped to Manhattan under the noses of the British fleet. By morning, all nine thousand members of his army had fled Brooklyn. Washington was in the last boat. The British had dealt the rebels a terrible blow, but Washington's calm and determined response prevented it from being fatal.

Revolutionaries often fail. Successful revolutionaries coolly pick up the pieces and fight on. Henry Heinz sold bottled horseradish as a boy and eventually started a processed food business. He did well until 1875, when fluctuations in produce prices drained his working capital and forced him into bankruptcy. But he didn't let the disaster stop him. He got a job, paid off his debts, and tried again. Soon he was running a new food company that grew into an international success.

Communication

A little neglect may breed mischief: for want of a nail the shoe was lost; for want of a shoe the horse was lost; and for want of a horse the rider was lost.

—BENJAMIN FRANKLIN

Bad Communication Compounds Disaster

Eighteenth-century communications were difficult at best. Battlefield communication was often impossible. Unit commanders knew the plan of battle beforehand but had to assume that things were proceeding as planned even when they did not know how events were unfolding elsewhere. When there was a major change in the situation that put the whole plan at risk, one wing of the army didn't always bother to warn the other. The results were often disastrous.

When the British began flanking the left wing of Washington's army during their attack on the Brooklyn Heights, Patriot officers didn't warn the rest of the army. The right wing only learned of their dire situation when the British attacked them from the rear. The failure to pass on information almost destroyed the Continental Army. Not communicating could easily wreck your revolution too.

Communication is much more rapid and reliable now. But it has its own set of problems. Patriot generals at least listened when a courier rode up with a message. Communication today is so voluminous that important messages are still lost. During a strategy session at Electronic Data Systems Corporation, two different units both reported that they were working on major transaction settlement systems for the energy industry. The units shared a building and customers, but they had missed the opportunity to cooperate effectively because fundamental messages were not exchanged. Even with the latest technology, communication still requires consistent, conscious effort.

Winning Strategies

If, to please the people, we offer what we ourselves disapprove, how can we afterward defend our work? Let us raise a standard to which the wise and honest can repair.

—George Washington

Washington Changes Strategy, 1776

After General Howe's victory on Long Island, his brother, Admiral Lord Richard Howe, sent for Patriot leaders to negotiate an end to the rebellion. Admiral Howe was certain that when confronted with the overwhelming British military advantage, the rebels could be persuaded to submit. Congress sent Benjamin Franklin, John Adams, and Edward Rutledge to negotiate. But to Howe's surprise, the Americans refused to abandon their fight for independence.

George Washington was equally adamant against giving in to British demands. He now understood it would be impossible to drive the British from America. The British could take any objective they chose with their superior force. But he was beginning to develop a strategy for winning the war.

Washington realized that King George would only be able to maintain control through overwhelming force. But even the mighty British army could not occupy the whole country against its will. Without local support for the Crown, American Patriots would reassert control as soon as British armies marched away. Or, they could—if a nucleus of resistance remained. That nucleus had to be Washington's army. As he wrote to Congress:

> *I am sensible that a retreating army is encircled with difficulties; that declining an engagement subjects a general to reproach: but when the fate of America may be at stake on the issue, we should protract the war, if possible.*

Washington changed the strategy for winning the war. Instead of the impossible task of driving the British from America, he crafted a new plan. Washington would keep his army together, even if it meant abandoning American towns and loyal patriots to the British. He did not need to control territory or crush the British war machine. His army just had to survive. It was not a glorious strategy, but it worked. The British won most of the battles of the Revolution. But they were never able to reverse American independence outside of the areas occupied by their armies.

Washington was not a timid or conservative general. He fought with great audacity when he needed to do so. But he was as pragmatic as he was bold. He judiciously selected the strategies that would win, regardless of whether they were bold, popular, or cautious.

It takes a great leader to select the tough strategy that will succeed. Many would rather go down in a blaze of glory than retrench their expectations. But winning is still winning, even if it takes longer. And losing is always losing, no matter how valiant the effort.

> In the late 1990s, the telecommunications industry was embroiled in revolutionary changes in the transmission market. Everyone correctly believed that the demand for fiberoptic and other high capacity transmission systems would grow rapidly. Many companies spent billions building extensive networks far in advance of demand. Others, like Verizon, were uncomfortable with the risks of such aggressive investment. They moderated spending to keep pace with demand. Their conservative approach was derided as foolish and shortsighted at the time, but as the bankruptcies of their more aggressive competitors later showed, winning is what matters.

Leadership Makes the Difference

*I hope I shall always possess firmness
and virtue enough to maintain what I consider
the most enviable of all titles, the character
of an honest man.*

—GEORGE WASHINGTON

Manhattan, September 1776

After negotiations in New York broke down, the British invaded Manhattan at Kip's Bay to complete the destruction of Washington's small army. It was another textbook operation carried out with overwhelming force. British frigates sailed in close to American positions and blasted the Patriots with cannon. Men were buried in their trenches from the fierce barrage while grapeshot cut down soldiers who tried to shoot back. British troops then landed and swept away what little resistance remained. The Patriots turned and ran for their lives. Washington could not stop them. His staff had to restrain him from attacking the British himself in frustration.

The Continental Army left a trail of abandoned muskets, powder horns, and mess pots. Most escaped, slipping through the heavy woods of Manhattan. Their retreat was aided by the great charm of Mary Lindley Murray, a dedicated and vivacious Patriot. General Howe stopped at her house for refreshment. She chatted with the general for hours while the Continental Army limped away. By the time Howe tore himself away from tea with his beautiful and witty hostess, the danger was past. Had the British chase been vigorous, the Continental Army would have been destroyed.

The Americans retreated to Harlem Heights. They had lost much of their baggage, cannon, and ammunition, but they had not lost their spirit. Men found their regiments, ate a meager meal and endured a cold, rainy night without blankets or tents. Washington formed a defensive line and the next day sent a detachment of Connecticut rangers to scout for the British. The rangers ran into several advancing British units, including the Forty-Second Royal Highlanders, the famous Black Watch. The two groups fought until the outnumbered Americans pulled back to keep from being flanked.

The British believed they had the rebels on the run again and blew hunting bugles to signal that the chase was on. Their contempt infuriated the Americans. Washington ordered reinforcements to join the fight. With this added strength, the Americans counterattacked. It wasn't a disciplined maneuver. The Patriots refused to do anything but advance and fire. But their attack was so fierce that the cream of the British army turned and ran.

The same army fought very differently on two consecutive days. They were beaten from the start at Kip's Bay. At Harlem Heights, they acquitted themselves bravely. The contrast is sharp, but hardly surprising. At Kip's Bay, the Continental Army could not win. If they had stood and fought, they would have been destroyed. When they fought the British again the next day, the Americans were fighting the freewheeling warfare in which they excelled. Even outnumbered, they dominated the British.

Leadership made the difference. In both cases, Washington and his staff picked the field of battle. The first day they chose the obvious, and wrong, battlefield. That choice just about lost the war. The second day they selected a fight where their troops could win, and win they did. Soldiers know when their leaders have put them in a strong position. They also understand when their leaders expect them to save an untenable situation. If you want your army to fight, put it in the strongest possible position. You may still be outnumbered and outgunned, but your soldiers must know that they have every possible advantage you can offer them.

World-renowned quality expert Edward Deming maintained that a company's system of doing business is responsible for eighty-five percent of a worker's effectiveness. The Revolution supports his claim. Incompetent leaders repeatedly squandered lives and battles. But when Patriots were led well, they performed stunning feats of arms.

In 1997, Steve Jobs again took the helm of troubled Apple Computer, Inc. Its small market share made Apple computers more costly and slower than competing Windows- and Intel-based computers. Heroic efforts by Apple employees could not close the gap. So Jobs adroitly redirected Apple development energies to areas where they could win. His iMac computers strongly differentiated Apple products. Their style and ease of use were right on target with core Apple customers. The integrated design supported lower retail prices by simplification and feature reduction. The iMac was perfectly suited to Apple's strengths.

Obsolete Tactics

*He's the best physician that knows
the worthlessness of the most medicines.*

—BENJAMIN FRANKLIN,
Poor Richard's Almanack 1733

Retreat from New York, 1776

Bunker Hill almost proved fatal to the Revolution. The famous battle taught Americans that they could beat the British, but it also enamored them of an obsolete strategy. In the New York campaign, the British took advantage of the Patriots' Bunker Hill mentality to repeatedly flank and destroy fortified American positions.

Washington's army withdrew from Manhattan to White Plains. There they dug in and waited for a British frontal attack, just like at Bunker Hill. Instead, the British flanked their lines and forced the Americans to withdraw into New Jersey. General Nathanael Greene left three thousand Patriot troops behind at Fort Washington on Manhattan Island. Greene was confident that his entrenched soldiers could repeat the carnage of Bunker Hill if the British attacked.

Greene was wrong. The British assault on Fort Washington was meticulously planned and executed. They easily captured the garrison with its three thousand men, one hundred and sixty cannon, and critical stores of powder. Then the British crossed the Hudson and quickly took Fort Lee and more critical stores. Much of the army Washington worked so hard to build was lost, along with most of the Patriot cannon, powder, and provisions. The men of the Continental Army were hungry, demoralized, and fleeing for their lives.

It is easy to learn the wrong lesson. The Quaker Oats Company was criticized for paying too much when it bought Gatorade for $240 million. Gatorade sales were then under $100 million. Quaker silenced critics by building Gatorade into a billion-dollar brand. But Gatorade was a dangerous precedent. It emboldened Quaker to pay too much for the Snapple brand, an acquisition that Quaker unloaded three years later at a $1.4 billion loss.

Hang On

Nothing can stop the man with the right mental attitude from achieving his goal; nothing on earth can help the man with the wrong mental attitude.

—THOMAS JEFFERSON

New Jersey, 1776

The British pursued Washington's army across New Jersey. Washington was not a coward, as he demonstrated on numerous occasions. But his army was on the brink of annihilation. He had to escape and rebuild. There was hope for the rebellion, even if it was hard to envision. Support for the Patriot cause was growing. British brutality convinced more and more Americans that independence was essential, and the Patriots had fought well despite their strategic blunders. No European army of conscripts and mercenaries could have survived the punishment that Washington's army had taken. Washington's strategy of maintaining an armed resistance would work if his army survived 1776. The Patriots had to hang on.

Even great innovators often must hang on until the time is right. William Boeing knew that aviation was the future. But after World War I, that future was slow in coming for his new company. Orders for new airplanes dried up. There was no work for Boeing's skilled craftsmen. He knew that business would bounce back. It would just take time. Boeing decided to hold on. He looked for other customers who could use their skills. Boeing built boats for fishermen and furniture for a corset maker and a confectioner. It might not seem like the right business for an aviation revolutionary, but the work kept Boeing's skilled workers employed until more aircraft orders could be found. Boeing hung on until the future caught up.

Reining in Geniuses

It is hard for an empty sack to stand upright.

—Benjamin Franklin,
The Way to Wealth, 1758

General Charles Lee

While a revolution often must tolerate a leader's learning, it cannot afford insubordination and dissension even in a promising general. After Charleston, General Charles Lee was given command of key units of Washington's army. Lee was the most experienced officer in the very green Continental officer corps. He received the credit for the Patriot victory at Charleston while many blamed Washington for the American defeats in New York.

Believing only his military genius could save the Revolution, Lee decided to maintain a separate command from Washington. He ignored orders to reinforce Washington when the Continental Army was in danger of being destroyed during the retreat through New Jersey in 1776. Fortunately for the Revolution, the British captured Lee while away from his command at an inn run by a pretty innkeeper. His successor marched to Washington's aid in time to prevent the army from coming apart.

Lee had started the revolution as one of its most promising leaders. He had solid military experience. Washington and others had a high opinion of his skill. However, over the course of the war, his vanity and insistence on independence destroyed his effectiveness. The Revolution was better off without his genius.

Hubris often nullifies genius. Michael Cimino was a gifted director. After proving his talent scripting *Silent Running* and directing *Thunderbolt and Lightfoot,* Cimino took almost three years to craft *The Deer Hunter.* It won Best Picture and four other Academy Awards in 1978. United Artists gave Cimino complete freedom for his next project, *Heaven's Gate.* Costs exploded as Cimino shot many times the usual footage on detailed, historically accurate sets. Worse, too much of that footage was kept. The finished film was released without prior screening at 219 minutes. It was pulled a few days later, edited and rereleased in a 150-minute version that also flopped. *Heaven's Gate* wrecked United Artists, which was bought out by MGM, and it almost destroyed the Western movie genre. Even genius is intolerable if it won't be subjected to controls.

Physical Stamina

To lengthen thy life, lessen thy meals.

—BENJAMIN FRANKLIN,
Poor Richard's Almanack 1733

Washington's Energetic Leadership

Washington had two important advantages as a general. First, he seemed to be bulletproof. Musket volleys and cannon fire couldn't touch him, even though he was repeatedly in the thick of battle during two wars. Bullets pierced his uniform, but he wasn't injured. One renowned British sharpshooter could have shot him, but inexplicably declined to fire. Not everyone can be so lucky, but most can enjoy Washington's other advantage, stamina. His physical stamina was essential to his ability to command. He didn't have the large, efficient staffs or experienced officer corps of his British opponents. He often almost had to lead the army personally. He saw to supplies, arranged transportation, reformed scattered units and directed combat. Washington's personal attention to detail repeatedly saved the army during the campaign of 1776.

The Continental Army retreated across New Jersey toward the Delaware River. Washington had the foresight to gather all of the boats along the Delaware. Through tireless work, he got all of his army and baggage across the river before the pursuing British could catch them. Without boats, General Howe decided to break off his pursuit and settle his army into winter quarters. Washington's army was safe.

Washington's incredibly good health allowed him to lead so effectively through eight long years of war. He loved vigorous exercise in the open air. And he took full advantage of meals with his officers and the rare party or ball to find relief from the pressures of command. Because of his good health and habits, Washington maintained his vigorous, energetic leadership through a grueling war that killed many lesser men.

Overseeing the dramatic expansion in research that filled Merck's product pipeline and led to its explosive growth was more than a full-time job for former Merck & Co., Inc. CEO Roy Vagelos. But Vagelos regularly made time to run five miles, play tennis, or row a single scull. Like innovative research, an investment in good health can pay spectacular dividends in energetic leadership.

Tolerate Learning

Tis easy to see, hard to foresee.

—BENJAMIN FRANKLIN

Washington Learns to Command

The Continental Army's performance during most of 1776 was a disaster and Washington made tactical and strategic mistakes that compounded the huge inadequacies of his army. It lost most of its men, powder, and cannon.

If Washington had reported the disasters of the campaign in many of today's organizations, he would have been fired. He probably would have been sacked if the Continental Congress had been functional. Reorganization was a very old remedy for failure, even in 1776. As the Greek philosopher Petronius Arbiter noted in 210 B.C.:

> *We trained hard, but it seemed that every time we were beginning to form up into teams, we would be reorganized. I was to learn in later life that we tend to meet any new situation by reorganizing, and a wonderful method it can be for creating the illusion of progress while producing confusion, inefficiency, and demoralization.*

Replacing Washington would have been a disaster. He made mistakes, but he also learned from them. Through the missteps, Washington was building an organization that he could work with and that would win the war. Washington now understood what could and couldn't be done with his amateur soldiers. His men and officers were training on the job. Issues of supply, communication, and political control were worked out as the war advanced. Washington was succeeding, even as he was losing battle after battle. Fortunately, Washington's education as commander in chief was tolerated. He was the only one with the military aptitude, leadership skills, and democratic spirit needed to win the war.

Failure is not necessarily incompetence. If your leader is laboring under impossible circumstances and has the confidence of his organization, let him learn from his mistakes. You may not have the right leader now, but you are making one the fastest way possible. Daniel Snyder founded student magazine *CampusUSA* with three million dollars from real estate developer and publisher Mortimer Zuckerman. The venture went bust, but Zuckerman recognized that Snyder was a winner. Zuckerman backed him again in a new venture, marketing firm Snyder Communications, which was a great success.

Groom New Talent

Issue the orders Sir, and I will storm hell.

—PATRIOT GENERAL ANTHONY WAYNE

Washington Builds an Officer Corps

The Continental Congress commissioned eight generals to lead the rebellion in 1775. All but one had served in the Seven Years' War years earlier. They were good initial choices, but few were active in important roles by the end of the revolution.

Washington won the war with a new generation of leaders. Most started the war with little military experience. The Marquis de Lafayette joined Washington's staff when barely out of his teens. But he was respectful, modest, and a fast learner. Washington soon depended on him to lead critical campaigns.

Nathanael Greene bought a book of military history and a gun when war threatened. He had no military experience, but he learned quickly. He became indispensable to Washington and ended the war with an independent command driving the British from the south.

Anthony Wayne began his military career as Colonel of a new regiment in 1776. His bravery earned him a promotion to general the next year. Washington would rely on Wayne's efficient courage throughout the war and his presidency.

Never neglect growing your next generation of stars. In 1989, the Minnesota Vikings traded twelve players and draft picks to the Dallas Cowboys for Herschel Walker, the star the Vikings believed they needed to win a Super Bowl. Walker was unable to win a Super Bowl for Minnesota, but Dallas developed the new talent it got from the deal into a team that won three Super Bowls.

Practice Makes Perfect

An advantage itinerant preachers have over those who are stationary, the latter cannot well improve their delivery of a sermon by so many rehearsals.

—Benjamin Franklin

The State Constitutions

Soon after the states declared themselves free of British rule, they created their own constitutions to replace their royal charters. Virginia was one of the first. Its constitution provided for a House of Delegates, elected annually, and a Senate, whose members stood for election every four years. It also mandated a governor, but his powers were sharply limited. Virginia had suffered much under Royal Governor John Murray before he had been driven from the state. Virginians made certain that future governors had less control.

Other states followed Virginia's example, adopting strong legislatures and weak governors. The new governments were not effective in supporting the war. The supreme legislatures were unable to act decisively, and the governors were prohibited from independent action. Thomas Jefferson's later experience as governor was typical. He was forbidden from taking vital steps to defend Virginia from a British invasion in 1781. A relatively weak British force devastated the state because there was no strong executive branch to organize resistance.

Massachusetts created its constitution several years after most of the other states, and it learned from their experience. John Adams produced most of the document. Adams was a diligent student of government. He recognized that although giving the people's legislature direct control of government seemed like a good idea, there were advantages to tempering legislative control. His constitution gave the executive and judicial branches of government independent power. Adams's governor was popularly elected and had a veto over legislation. The governor was also the commander in chief of the state's armed forces and appointed state officials.

Adams's constitution wasn't as idealistically democratic as earlier state constitutions, but by learning from their experiences he was able to make government more effective. The other states eventually followed Adams's model.

Experience can improve on even the best ideas. Leon Leonwood Bean knew he had the perfect boot for sportsmen when he combined waterproof galoshes with comfortable leather uppers. But ninety of the first one hundred pairs he sold were returned because the rubber and leather halves of the boot were separating. Bean used that unpleasant incident to improve his design until the two halves stayed together. Experience made the perfect boot perfect and L.L. Bean rich.

Having a Stake

The God who gave us life, gave us liberty
at the same time.

—THOMAS JEFFERSON

The Voting Franchise

The framers of the first state constitutions believed that voting citizens needed to have a stake in their society. Most states allowed male taxpayers to vote. Others required a citizen to own property.

These requirements were often used by local oligarchies to maintain political control. In New York, the property requirement was high. Many otherwise hardworking, taxpaying New Yorkers were denied suffrage until Aaron Burr found a loophole in the voting laws in 1800. New York at that time required voters to have one hundred dollars in property, a requirement Burr manipulated by helping poor New Yorkers collectively purchase one hundred dollars worth of property and then register it individually. The tactic proved legal and eventually led to a shift in the balance of power and later a change in the law. Still, almost all the Founders in their various state constitutions insisted that a stake in the community was a precondition to the voting franchise. Otherwise, they feared that voters would decide against the best interests of their states.

We now consider residence in our communities a sufficient interest for voting rights, but having a financial stake is still important. Any organization is more flexible when members have a strong interest in its success. In 1999, a blizzard shut down Detroit Metropolitan Airport. The storm interrupted the standard procedures for parking and unloading planes. Worse, rigid rules and policies kept Northwest Airlines's ground crews from improvising alternatives for getting passengers off the planes. Other airlines were deplaning passengers. But without the motivation to bend rules in a crisis, Northwest crews left almost four thousand passengers stuck on planes until conditions returned to normal.

Deferring Change

Force cannot change right.

— Thomas Jefferson,
to Major John Cartwright, 1824

Jefferson's Bill for Religious Freedom

Thomas Jefferson left the Continental Congress in 1776. He declined an appointment to represent the new nation in Paris and returned home to care for his family and to help organize the government of the Commonwealth of Virginia. As part of his work, Jefferson drafted a revolutionary statute for religious freedom in 1777. It prevented government from forcing citizens to support a religion and allowed the free practice of beliefs without the loss of civil rights.

Jefferson's bill was a brilliant, far-sighted work, but the time wasn't right for it. Dominant religions still had great power in all the states except Rhode Island and Connecticut. Even in easygoing Virginia, people were not ready for so radical a change. Jefferson wisely dropped his bill. It took time for Virginians to become comfortable with religious freedom, but eventually they were ready. Jefferson's statute for religious freedom was adopted in 1785.

Sometimes even great ideas have to wait. Mahlon Loomis demonstrated the first wireless telegraph transmission in New York in 1868, but the primitive technical infrastructure made it difficult to finance the development of a radio revolution. Loomis returned to his dental practice. Radio would have to wait another generation until more advanced electronics and widespread electrical power allowed Guglielmo Marconi to pioneer wireless communications again.

Experimentation

*It is better to correct error while new and
before it becomes inveterate by habit and custom.*

—THOMAS JEFFERSON,
IN A 1777 REPORT TO CONGRESS

Pennsylvania's Radical Government

The new Pennsylvania state government was the boldest experiment in government among the states. The constitution, drafted by George Bryan and Thomas Young with help from Benjamin Franklin, was designed to give citizens the greatest possible control over their government. It mandated a single legislative house, with representatives elected every year. There were term limits. A representative could only serve four of seven years. The president of the state was also elected annually, but the real power resided in the legislature.

The Pennsylvania experiment quickly became the Founders' prime example of the dangers of complete democracy. Many Pennsylvanians had chafed under Quaker domination of the colony. The dissidents took control of the new government and quickly disenfranchised most of the Quakers by mandating a loyalty oath that the Quakers refused to take. During the war, this fiercely democratic government spent more of its energies plundering the estates of wealthy loyalists and prosecuting conscientious objectors than supporting the war effort. Pennsylvania finally abandoned its experiment in raw democracy in 1790, adopting a two-house legislature and a strong governor.

It is not surprising that Franklin's Pennsylvania would have tried such a bold experiment. Benjamin Franklin was an intensely curious experimenter. His experiments led him to invent swim fins, rocking chairs, a catheter, and a haunting musical instrument, the glass armonica. He charted the Gulf Stream, proposed Daylight Saving Time, and determined the most efficient routes for carrying the mail by measuring distances with an odometer of his own design.

Like the Pennsylvania Constitution of 1776, not all of his experiments succeeded at first. Franklin was certain there had to be a better way to heat a room than with a fireplace. He designed a metal box that proved a more efficient fireplace because it was entirely in the room. However, Franklin's Pennsylvania Fireplace leaked smoke into the room because it drew poorly. David Rittenhouse finally corrected Franklin's design with an L-shaped chimney, making the Franklin Stove one of history's most popular inventions.

Experiments are invaluable, even when they fail. Bob Kierlin decided to put bolts and other industrial fasteners in a vending machine so construction and industrial customers could get them whenever they needed them. Unfortunately, the fasteners customers wanted most didn't always fit in a vending machine. But the experiment inspired Kierlin to open a fastener store. Today his company, Fastenal, has hundreds of high-margin retail outlets because he was willing to try something unusual.

CHAPTER SIX

WINNING

✴ ✴ ✴

Taking Big Chances

Speculation, peculation and an insatiable thirst
for riches seem to have got the better of every other
consideration and almost of every order of men.

—GEORGE WASHINGTON

Risk-Taking in America

The Americans of 1776 were great risk-takers. They had to be. All aspects of eighteenth-century life were uncertain. Homesteading raw land was a huge gamble. If settlers survived they could still lose their farms after years of sacrifice when civilization reached them and conflicting ownership claims were sorted out. But even those who stayed in the more settled areas ran risks just running a farm or engaging in a trade. Economic fluctuations were severe because of the shortage of money. Debt often took the place of cash. And anyone who couldn't pay his debts could be dragged off to prison until the debt was paid—never an easy thing to do from behind bars.

The greatest uncertainty Americans faced was the constant risk of death. Average Americans were better fed, better clothed, and better housed than almost any people in the world in 1776, but most still died while they were relatively young. Disaster was so familiar that Americans preferred the risks that could improve their lives to the risks of venturing nothing.

Sometimes risk is the safest course. Philip Armour made his first fortune taking a big chance. He contracted to sell pork at irresistibly low prices, betting that the American Civil War would end and prices would drop before he had to deliver. Prices did drop, bankrupting competitors. Armour got rich. After winning that gamble, he took a bigger one, betting that he could do meatpacking more efficiently from large central-ized facilities, competing against local butchers. Armour's higher productivity wiped out most small competitive opera-tions. Smart risks are often safer than taking no risks at all.

Show You Can Win

He that lives upon hope will die fasting.

—BENJAMIN FRANKLIN

Little Victories Pave the Way for Big Victories

By the end of 1776, the Continental Army was on the brink of dissolu-tion. The British had just driven them from New York and New Jersey.

They were already badly outnumbered. And the ill-fed, badly clothed troops were ready to quit when their enlistments ended with the year.

Washington needed a victory. Without a success to boost the morale of his troops and Patriot civilians, the army would collapse. Washington concluded he had to strike at the British.

It was a bold gamble. Even moving his frozen, hungry troops was risky. But Washington's spies revealed that the British army was spread widely in order to provide comfortable winter quarters for all of their troops. He would strike at the edges of the British position—Trenton, Bordentown, and Burlington—on Christmas night.

Washington personally led the attack on Trenton. A cold, bitter storm sorely tried the ill-clad Patriot troops as they crossed the ice-choked Delaware and marched through the long night. But the weather kept the British and Hessians indoors. Although the Patriot army arrived at Trenton far behind schedule, they still hadn't been detected. The British and Hessian troops had turned out for morning formations and gone back to bed. Washington's attack was a stunning success. His shivering army marched out of the cold and captured almost the entire garrison. There were few American casualties.

Washington withdrew from Trenton. Learning that the Bordentown and Burlington attacks had been aborted, he decided he needed one more victory to keep his army together. He again crossed the Delaware and took up positions at Trenton. General Charles Cornwallis marched to meet him. Washington wanted a victory more than a fight. He eluded Cornwallis during the night, leaving a few men behind to tend hundreds of campfires. Marching to Princeton, Washington conspicuously led his men against the British. The British line broke and Washington urged his troops on to complete the route. He then prudently retreated to the defensible heights of Morristown before the main British army could engage his hungry, exhausted troops.

Washington's victories did not materially slow the British military machine. The British still had overwhelming superiority. Cornwallis was probably right when he declared that if Washington tried to attack again, "the march alone will destroy his army." But the victories were enough to impress both friend and foe. Patriots would fight on because they knew they could win.

> Show that your organization is a winner. Even demonstration victories lead to success. Hyundai had steadily improved the quality of its cars in the 1990s. But better quality hadn't translated into increased sales. It was hard to change the perceptions of dealers and customers. Hyundai needed a dramatic demonstration to show it was a winner. In 1999, they decided to highlight their quality by offering one hundred thousand-mile warranties. It was a bold move, but it demonstrated that Hyundai believed in its product. Sales jumped seventy percent in the next two years.

Micro/Macro Mismanagement

Power always thinks it has a great soul and
vast views beyond the comprehension of the weak.

—JOHN ADAMS,
IN A LETTER TO HIS WIFE, ABIGAIL, 1780

Orders for the Hudson Campaign of 1777

The head of the war effort in Britain, Lord George Germain, decided to cut the rebellious colonies in two by sending General Howe north along the Hudson from New York City while directing General Burgoyne to march south from Canada, across Lake Champlain and down the Hudson to link with Howe. It was a good plan. Patriot leaders were also fearful of their ability to continue the war if the British divided the states.

To put his plan in motion, Germain sent a letter to General Howe suggesting that Howe march up the Hudson to join General Burgoyne, who would march south from Canada. However, Germain, who resided in England, decided to personally direct Burgoyne's campaign from across the Atlantic. He ordered Burgoyne to split his force in two, with one column attacking westward across New York and the other driving south from Montreal. He also mandated that Burgoyne employ his Native American allies. Germain's strategy of taking the Hudson Valley and dividing the colonies in two could have worked if all three British columns had attacked, but overly vague orders to Howe and the micromanagement of Burgoyne resulted in disaster.

Howe ignored Germain's suggestion. He didn't send any troops up the Hudson until it was too late. If Germain had made Howe's orders clear when they were delivered and in follow-up dispatches, the outcome could have been much different.

Burgoyne did exactly as he was told, and his campaign suffered for it. He organized two invasion forces. Colonel Barry St. Leger attacked from the west across New York and besieged Fort Stanwix. His force turned back when Benedict Arnold arrived with relief force at the fort. St. Leger's withdrawal deprived Burgoyne of much-needed reinforcements and provisions. Burgoyne led the other column himself. Against his own better judgment, he took along bands of Native Americans as Germain ordered. The Indians committed atrocities including the murder of a young woman, Jane McCrea, which quickly united the entire region against Burgoyne's army. But the Native Americans were only in the campaign for plunder. They wisely melted away as the enraged local militias began to close in on the British. By the end of the summer, there was only one British army in upstate New York, and it was in trouble.

Leaders are often tempted to meddle in the jobs of their subordinates while ignoring the responsibilities that only they can do. E.F. Hutton imploded in the mid-1980s because there was no executive management in key areas and too much in others. Hutton's CEO, Robert Fomon, allowed top executives great latitude over their budgets and ethics. Costs ballooned while several key executives were involved in a check-kitting scandal, moving funds between accounts while collecting the interest, that seriously damaged Hutton's reputation. But at the same time, Fomon was micromanaging much of the organization, personally setting salaries for more than one thousand employees and making minor budget and planning decisions for numerous departments. Because of Fomon's misplaced management, Hutton collapsed and was bought out by Shearson at a bargain price.

Too Cautious to Win

I heard the bullets whistle, and believe me, there is something charming in the sound.

—GEORGE WASHINGTON

New Jersey, 1777

Washington's spectacular victories at Trenton and Princeton did more than save Patriot morale. They clouded General Howe's judgment. After being humiliated by the Patriots, Howe felt he had to crush Washington's army to restore his honor. But he also moved with great care, fearing being tricked again by the Patriot general. His caution doomed the British offensive in 1777. Howe repeatedly maneuvered to crush Washington, but the Patriot general slipped out of all his overly careful traps.

Howe concluded that the only way to bring Washington to a decisive confrontation was to threaten Philadelphia, the rebel capital. The city was only sixty miles away, but Howe feared leaving the coast and his lifeline to the Royal Navy. So he abandoned New Jersey to Washington, giving the Patriots another victory. Howe was so fearful of losing to Washington that it became impossible for him to win.

> Fixating on a competitor can lead to disaster. Compaq got its start competing against IBM for the PC market. The rivalry intensified over the years, especially over quality. Compaq spent millions of dollars building computers that were as good or better than IBM's. But Compaq was so fearful of losing to IBM that it lost sight of where the PC market was going. Lower-priced competitors began undercutting both IBM and Compaq. Only when faced with huge losses did Compaq shift to lower-priced PCs, a move that allowed it to finally take the PC market share crown from IBM.

Decisive Action

*They would not believe themselves in danger
until they found ruin at their doors.*

—NATHANAEL GREENE, PATRIOT GENERAL,
IN A LETTER TO COLONEL JOSEPH REED, MARCH 18, 1781

The Armies Move to Philadelphia, 1777

Howe loaded his army onto sweltering transport ships while he decided what he should do next. His fast, water-borne army could have overwhelmed almost any strategic objective before Washington could arrive to check him. But Howe squandered his advantage, delaying while he agonized over his options.

Howe's indecision gave Washington time to prepare to follow the British. He knew from his spies that Howe was supposed to advance up the Hudson, but could also strike Philadelphia. Washington prepared to act instantly against either move. When British ships were sighted off the capes of Delaware, Washington guessed that Howe would attack the Patriot capital. He immediately marched his army to protect Philadelphia. When Howe finally landed his army in Maryland and advanced on Philadelphia, Washington was waiting for him. Washington's decisive action nullified the British advantage of quick movement.

Decisive action can overcome a host of disadvantages. Jay Gould made a fortune by acting with speed. Railroads were consolidating to raise rates. When Gould heard competitors were putting together a monopoly, he immediately bought minor rail lines that together offered an alternative to the new monopoly. Gould then sold out to the monopoly or took a cut of its profits himself. It was a simple plan. He made it work by acting decisively when an opportunity presented itself.

Skepticism

The used key is always bright.

—BENJAMIN FRANKLIN,
Poor Richard Improved

Brandywine, September 9–11, 1777: The Maneuvering

Washington deployed his army along the Brandywine River at Chad's Ford to block Howe's advance toward Philadelphia. It was an advantageous position on high ground along the road between Baltimore and Philadelphia. Washington also guarded nearby fords to prevent the British from flanking him. The Continental Army was in a strong position to stop the British at the river.

Howe decided against following a frontal assault. A Loyalist told him of an undefended ford far to the north. He had a portion of his army make obvious preparations for an attack on the Americans at Chad's Ford while he personally led the bulk of his army to the vulnerable crossing. Washington received contradictory reports of Howe's movements, some warning of the British flanking action, others claiming they were only feinting north. The energetic British activity and faulty intelligence reports from Patriot scouts convinced Washington that the main attack would come at Chad's Ford. Washington did not shift his army to meet this rumored threat.

Howe had flanked Washington enough times in the past that Washington should have been more skeptical of his own intelligence. Flanking was Howe's favorite maneuver. Even expert local scouts could be mistaken. Washington almost lost his army because he wasn't skeptical of the information he received.

> Daniel Ludwig had no doubts about turning more than six thousand square miles of Amazon jungle into a private pulp and paper empire. But there were reasons to be skeptical. Ludwig had to float in a massive seventeen-story pulp mill from Japan, build a deep-water port, construct thousands of miles of roads, and plant two hundred and sixty thousand acres of trees before collecting the first dime of revenue. Ludwig's lack of skepticism doomed the project. He invested hundreds of millions of dollars before discovering the plan's fatal flaws, including that the trees he planted wouldn't survive the local climate. Ludwig had to abandon his Amazon empire, and in 1999 banks offered it for sale for one dollar, plus its $345 million of debt.

Learning from Defeat

There are more old drunkards than old doctors.

—BENJAMIN FRANKLIN

Brandywine, September 11, 1777: The Battle

Howe crossed the Brandywine and marched south to flank the Patriot army. Washington finally learned that he had been fooled and set up a hasty defensive line. The British repeatedly broke the American line, but the Patriots quickly fell back, reformed their line, and fought on. Nathanael Greene led a regiment on a four-mile dash to fill a key gap, preventing the British from overwhelming the Patriot army. But as American units shifted to meet Howe, the balance of the British forces surged across the Brandywine at Chad's Ford, driving the Americans back along a second front.

Brandywine was almost the decisive battle Howe had hoped for. However, the Continental Army did not collapse. It made a fighting withdrawal toward Philadelphia and escaped after dark. The Patriots actually emerged from the battle more confident than ever. They knew they had fought well, and next time they would avoid their Brandywine mistakes.

Defeat can show the way to victory. Walt Disney's first commercial success was a cartoon about a lovable character, Oswald the Lucky Rabbit. But Disney had sold the rights to Oswald to his distributor, who decided to make the Oswald films himself. Disney's experience was painful, but not fatal. Knowing he could succeed, Disney retained the rights to his next lovable character, Mickey Mouse, who soon generated a fortune in film, book, and toy revenues.

More than You Bargain for

The play, sir, is over.

—MARQUIS DE LAFAYETTE

Lafayette's Serial Revolutionary Career

One casualty of note during the Battle of Brandywine was the Marquis de Lafayette, who was shot in the leg. Lafayette had just arrived in America and was serving as Washington's *aide-de-camp*. The young French nobleman was rich and powerful but not contented with his almost perfect life. Lafayette longed for the excitement of a revolution. He should have been more careful what he wished for. The Marquis was to be embroiled in great revolutions for the next fifty years.

The Marquis de Lafayette, with a promise of a major general's commission in the Continental Army, bought a ship and sailed to America. General Washington allowed the nineteen-year-old Frenchman to join his staff. He knew the political value of having a well-connected French nobleman on his side. He soon recognized Lafayette's loyalty, bravery, and leadership. Lafayette served with great distinction. He was recognized in America and in France as one of the great heroes of the war.

After returning to France, Lafayette worked to establish a constitutional monarchy. He was given command of the revolutionary National Guard after the fall of the Bastille. His fellow revolutionaries turned against him when he fired on a mob during a violent insurrection. He fled France and was imprisoned by the Austrians.

Lafayette was repatriated by Napoleon. He became a member of the Chamber of Deputies. There he was part of a third revolution, forcing the abdication of Napoleon after the battle of Waterloo. However, Lafayette was still not done with revolution. He led an 1830 revolution that brought down the Bourbon monarchy. Many wanted him to become president of a new French republic, but instead Lafayette established a constitutional monarchy with Louis-Philippe as president. He probably would have been involved in a fifth revolution to replace Louis-Philippe if he had not died in 1834, a revolutionary to the end.

Roy Park was both a typical and revolutionary serial entrepreneur. Park got a job as a reporter to repay his brother after wrecking his car. After graduation, he worked in public relations at agricultural cooperatives. He acquired the advertising agency of the Grange League Federation, which had more than one hundred employees. A client asked him to find a name for their new product line. Park suggested Duncan Hines. The client didn't want the name, so Park used it himself and went into the packaged food business. Procter & Gamble eventually bought the business. Park advised P&G for several years and noticed that advertising dollars were shifting from newspapers to television. He promptly bought a TV station in Greenville, North Carolina. He soon acquired more stations. And then, to bring his career full circle, he started buying newspapers too.

You Never Know Which Battles Count

Live free or die. Death is not the worst of evils.

—JOHN STARK,
VETERAN OF BUNKER HILL AND PATRIOT GENERAL

Bennington, August 16, 1777

As Burgoyne advanced south, his army ran low on food. The British general couldn't move enough food through hundreds of miles of wilderness, and the Patriots under General Phillip Schuyler were actively destroying all provisions in the country ahead of the British march. Still, Burgoyne was confident. He loved campaigning, enjoying luxurious living, a bubbly mistress, and the excitement of conflict. All would be well if he could procure more food.

Hearing of a Patriot supply depot at Bennington in what is now Vermont, Burgoyne sent Colonel Friedrich Baum with a detachment to capture the provisions. A New Hampshire brigade under General John Stark met Baum. Stark was a distinguished veteran of Bunker Hill who had resigned his commission when a rival was promoted over him. He now served with the New Hampshire militia. Confronted with Stark's unexpected resistance, Baum dug in on a hill some miles from Bennington and sent for reinforcements.

Before help arrived, the Patriots stormed the British position. Stark led the attack, shouting, "You must beat them or tonight Molly Stark sleeps a widow." Fighting was fierce, but the Patriots flanked the British and overran the hill. The British relief force arrived soon after, but it was intercepted and mauled by a Patriot brigade from the Green Mountains who had come to join the fight. Burgoyne had lost much of his army. And without the Bennington supplies, the British were now in a desperate race. They had to break through the encircling Patriots before winter sealed their doom. One small battle proved to be pivotal in the war.

In the early 1980s, Intel and Motorola were competing to establish their microprocessor architectures. Motorola's architecture was designed into several prominent personal computers, including Apple, while Intel's microprocessor was included in more than 2,500 products as part of its Orange Crush campaign. None of these skirmishes mattered. IBM had designed a personal computer and chose the Intel chip because it had support components they needed. It may have seemed like another microprocessor skirmish, but it was in fact the whole war. The IBM PC architecture became the basis for the bulk of the computer industry. The Motorola architecture was used in many products, including the recent Palm Pilot, but only achieved a fraction of Intel's volume of sales.

Instant Reinforcements

Those that can give up essential liberty to obtain a little temporary safety deserve neither liberty nor safety.

—BENJAMIN FRANKLIN

Patriot Militias

One of the Patriots' few advantages over the British was their ability to call out local militias. Americans lacked the money to maintain large armies. The tiny standing armies that Washington and other generals did manage to hold together were never adequately supplied. But when the need was great, thousands of militia could be gathered to swell Patriot ranks. Militias allowed the Patriots to take on the massive British war machine at a price Americans could afford.

Militias had many disadvantages. They were undisciplined and unreliable. They often melted away during battle and in camp. But when properly handled, they won some spectacular victories. And most Americans preferred joining militias. They only wanted to be soldiers when there was a fight.

As Burgoyne's army marched south, the American forces in the area swelled with thousands of local militiamen. Schuyler tirelessly gathered men and cannon to defeat the invaders. A few weeks before, the American defenders had been outnumbered. Now, with thirteen thousand men to Burgoyne's seven thousand, the Patriots were the superior force.

> Businesses use outsourcing similar to Revolutionary militias, adding expertise and resources as they are needed. Microsoft has enormous technical capabilities. But when it began designing its Xbox video game system, it went to contract manufacturer Flextronics. Flextronics had manufacturing capacity and skill that Microsoft hadn't needed in the past and invaluable experience in similar designs. The outsourced expertise proved critical in getting Xbox to market.

Overcommitted and Far from Home

Experience keeps a dear school,
but fools will learn in no other.

—BENJAMIN FRANKLIN

New York, 1777

The Patriots blocked Burgoyne's route down the Hudson River. They also cut the tenuous British supply line into Canada. Winter was coming on and the British were running out of food. Realizing Burgoyne's peril, Howe finally ordered General Clinton to advance up the Hudson to relieve Burgoyne, but the move was too late. Burgoyne's efficient, professional army was simply overextended in unfamiliar territory. Defeat was certain.

Big commitments are a dangerous risk when operating far from familiar territory. Mattel made a strategic misstep when it purchased children's software publisher The Learning Company for $3.6 billion. Mattel's new CEO, Jill Barad, knew toys, having led the dramatic growth of the Barbie line. But Barad did not understand children's software or its channels. The Learning Company began hemorrhaging money. Mattel was overcommitted in a business it didn't understand. Jill Barad was soon gone and The Learning Company given away for no upfront cash to stop the losses.

It was not the first time that Mattel was burned in

unfamiliar territory. Almost two decades earlier, the company made another bold foray into the electronic game business, led by the executive responsible for the growth of its Hot Wheels toy racecar business. Mattel Electronics grew rapidly at first, but the video game market was quickly saturated with primitive games. Mattel was caught with huge inventories that it couldn't unload and was forced to sell a number of its subsidiaries to pay for the debacle.

Mobility

Both armies seemed determined to conquer or die.

—JOHN GLOVER, PATRIOT SOLDIER,
IN A LETTER TO JONATHAN GLOVER AND AZOR ORNE,
SEPTEMBER 21, 1777

Freeman's Farm, September 19, 1777

Burgoyne was determined to push through the Patriots to Albany, where he could link up with Clinton's relief force. On September 19, 1777, he struck the Americans at Freeman's Farm. The British attacked across a large field, but were stopped by Patriot forces protected by the trees on the other side. Benedict Arnold led a vicious counterattack. Fighting surged back and forth across the field while Americans moved through the forest to flank the British.

The rough terrain was ideal for the Americans because it gave them the advantage of mobility. In other battles, the American troops had been less mobile than their British foes. It took a disciplined, trained army to move and fire together under battlefield conditions. But here, the broken terrain made large unit movements difficult. Fighting and advancing in small groups, the Americans were mobile and deadly. They kept up a withering fire on the British for the rest of the day. The British held the field of battle, but at a terrible cost.

Mobility is crucial for business success too. Sears became a leading American retailer through mobility, selling mail order to isolated rural customers. But in the 1920s, the company's growth slowed as urbanization and automobiles made it easier for customers to reach centralized stores. Sears changed its formula for mobility, opening its chain of retail stores and igniting a second season of growth.

Aggression

I would not only fight them, but would attack them, for I hold it an established maxim that there is three to one in favor of the party attacking.

— ALEXANDER HAMILTON

Bemis Heights, October 7, 1777

Burgoyne ordered a last desperate attack to extract his army from the Patriot trap. The British would strike the Americans hard, and then pull back. Burgoyne expected the Patriot line to retreat, just like they had at their last engagement at Freeman's Farm. The new American commander, General Horatio Gates, who had replaced Schuyler, had allowed the British to be the aggressors in the campaign. Burgoyne counted on Gates to be cautious again. While the Americans regrouped, the British would slip around them. Before Gates could move to block him, Burgoyne planned to be on his way to Albany.

The British launched their attack late in the morning, but the Americans surprised them. Instead of just defending, they became the aggressors. Benedict Arnold rallied five regiments of Patriots to counterattack the British advance. Arnold pushed back the British advance and then assaulted their main lines. Patriots breached British positions in many places and would have captured the whole British army if darkness hadn't ended the fight. The British were beaten. Burgoyne began a hasty retreat the next day, finally digging in near Saratoga. On October 17, the British army surrendered.

> Acting aggressively changes the odds. William McGowan had a daring agenda when he took control of struggling Microwave Communications of America, Inc. in 1968. MCI, as it later became known, planned to build a private telephone network between major cities. But AT&T, the largest, most profitable telephony company in America, had no intention of giving up any of its monopoly. McGowan decided the best strategy was to be the aggressor. When Ma Bell refused to provide local connections for MCI's service, McGowan sued. After many expensive years, MCI won its case. When the AT&T breakup was ordered in 1982, MCI was in the best position to capitalize on the new competitive environment.

Get the Best

*If you expect people to be ignorant and free
you expect what never was and never will be.*

—THOMAS JEFFERSON

Hamilton Gets Reinforcement from Gates

Washington had sent some of his best troops north to help stop Burgoyne's invasion. After Saratoga, he sent Alexander Hamilton to retrieve them from Gates to bolster his own hard-pressed army. However, Gates refused to release the troops, even though Washington was his commanding officer. Gates was more interested in maintaining his own power than the common good. He faced no threat, but clung to every regiment in his command.

Hamilton persisted until Gates relented and offered to send his worst regiments. Hamilton might have claimed victory and ended his frustrating assignment, but he knew Washington needed the toughest soldiers in the army. He continued to press Gates until he got the best troops before returning to Washington.

Get the best for your organization. They are a bargain. King Gillette had been looking for a product that customers would buy, use, throw away, and buy again. He decided to pursue shaving, the first razor and blade strategy. However, Gillette could not find a way to make simple, cheap blades. He experimented for years without success. In desperation he turned to one the most brilliant inventors in America, Professor William Nickerson. Nickerson's services were expensive. But within two years he had solved the problem, allowing Gillette to put disposable blades on the market.

Keep It Simple

Three removes are as bad as a fire.

—BENJAMIN FRANKLIN

Germantown, October 4, 1777

With winter approaching, most of the British army under General Howe settled into winter quarters in Germantown near Philadelphia. Washington decided to make another unexpected attack. Germantown was fewer than twenty miles from his camp. He would march his army through the night and surprise the British at dawn.

Washington developed an elaborate strategy for the attack. The army would travel in four columns over different routes, some little more than byways. The columns were to arrive at Germantown and attack simultaneously. Washington loved complex battle plans. He repeatedly tried to execute complicated, coordinated attacks. But something always went wrong. Germantown was not to be an exception.

The attack began well. Although Washington's column arrived at Germantown during the day, a thick fog still gave the Patriots the element of surprise. Washington pushed to the edge of the British camp and heard fighting on his left where Greene's column had already engaged the British. Victory seemed within his grasp when the plan unraveled. Some of Greene's men ran out of ammunition and fled. Washington's troops panicked when they saw Greene's troops run and heard firing behind them. Washington and Greene's columns had stumbled into each other in the fog and exchanged shots. But fearing they had been surrounded, the advanced units turned and ran. Washington was unable to stop their flight and the battle was lost.

The other Patriot columns never did make it to the fight. They got lost along the way. Too much complexity had snarled American chances for a victory. Washington won when his strategy was simple, like at Princeton. There he marched his army straight to a situation where they had the advantage. The simplicity of the plan overcame the inevitable mix-ups and failures.

Simple plans are good plans. Motorola lost its position as the top mobile phone manufacturer because it pursued a complicated strategy. Industry leaders seldom lose market share quickly, since they have the resources to counter competitive threats. But Motorola tried to cover both analog and digital markets, offering a wide variety of phones in each. The strategy gave them far too many models to manage. They were unable to roll out improvements and maintain synergies in components and manufacturing. While Motorola was bogged down executing their complex strategy, Nokia focused on a few models of digital phones using the same components. Nokia's simple, focused strategy propelled it to the top.

Maintain Momentum

A slender acquaintance with the world must convince every man that actions, not words, are the true criterion of the attachment of friends.
—George Washington

Germantown: The Chew Mansion

Part of the Patriot attack at Germantown failed because it lost its momentum. British troops in the path of the Patriot advance withdrew to a large, sturdy house, the Chew Mansion. The Americans were unable to capture, burn or blast the house. Rebel commanders were reluctant to leave any enemy soldiers behind their lines. Rather than advance and take the fight to the rest of the still-confused British army, the American attack ground to a halt. The British had time to regroup and counterattack. By trying to tie up all their loose ends before advancing, the Patriots lost one of their best opportunities for victory.

When victory is in sight, don't lose momentum to details. J.R. Simplot built an extensive potato and onion processing business through hard work and gutsy entrepreneurial risk-taking. But shipping ten thousand boxcars of produce annually only netted Simplot a little over one dollar a car. In 1940, he happened to meet one of his produce customers' clients, who needed flaked, powdered, and dried onions. Simplot didn't know anything about processing onions, but he saw the chance to improve his profit margins. He agreed on the spot to supply the man with five hundred thousand pounds of processed onions and then drove off to learn how to do it. Living by his motto that "Nothing will ever be attempted if all possible objections must be first overcome" made him a billionaire.

The Right Foe

I do not know what effect these names have on the enemy, but I confess they make me tremble.

—MEMBER OF PARLIAMENT WILLIAM PITT,
ON THE BRITISH COMMANDERS SELECTED TO FIGHT
THE WAR IN AMERICA

General William Howe

The American Revolution probably would have been crushed except that an unusually lackluster group led the British war effort. Prime Minister Lord Frederick North hated the war and begged the King to dismiss him. John Montagu, Earl of Sandwich and First Lord of the Admiralty, worked hard to line his own pockets while neglecting the Royal Navy. But General William Howe gave the Revolution its biggest break. Howe was competent at organizing and moving his armies. He repeatedly outmaneuvered Washington. But Howe did not aggressively pursue and destroy the Continental Army. His inaction may have been influenced by his sympathy for the American cause, or by the pretty mistresses and lavish parties he enjoyed while not campaigning. Whatever the reason, Howe gave the infant revolution its chance to survive.

The revolution could have ended in 1776 if Britain had sent a tenacious general. American public opinion was only just turning to independence. A decisive performance on the battlefield by British troops would have put an early end to the rebellion. General Howe did not get the chance to settle his score with Washington. After a massive farewell party, General Henry Clinton replaced him in 1778.

Choose your competitors carefully. Arthur Blank and Bernie Marcus were investigating discounting for the Handy Dan home improvement chain when it was acquired. The new owners weren't interested in discounting, making them perfect competitors. Blank and Marcus started Home Depot. With a better selection and better prices, they started another retail revolution.

CHAPTER SEVEN

Teams and Allies

The Ultimate Compensation

Whenever you are to do a thing,
though it can never be known but to yourself,
ask yourself how you would act were all the world
looking at you, and act accordingly.

—THOMAS JEFFERSON

Inspiring Patriots to Serve

Washington served for the duration of the war without pay. He was as selfless as his hero, the Roman patriot Cincinnatus, who abandoned his plow and team to lead the armies of Rome. However, most recruits to the Continental Army wanted to be paid. They lobbied for land grants, the stock options of the eighteenth century, but they rarely got anything and suffered horribly from want of food and clothing. Still, many stayed with Washington to the end. They knew they were serving a great cause and made incredible sacrifices to see it through. There are more powerful incentives than money.

People crave the chance to make a difference. America Online received billions of dollars of volunteer support from people who wanted to be part of the online revolution. Volunteers received free time on AOL as partial compensation, but most put in hours monitoring chat rooms and managing content that far exceeded the meager value of their time online. They were proud of what they were doing and of the community they were building. The 2001 Randstad North American Employee Review found that ninety percent of employees equated true success on the job with being trusted to get the job done. Let your people feel proud of what they are doing, and they can do anything.

Setting an Example

These are the times that try men's souls.

—THOMAS PAINE

Valley Forge, 1777–78

After Germantown, Washington took his army into winter quarters at Valley Forge, Pennsylvania. His troops were hungry, ragged and exhausted from the 1777 campaign. It was a desperate time. Officers resigned their commissions. Soldiers decamped. Their privations, and those of their families, were too much to bear. Death and disease ravaged those who remained. Valley Forge threatened to become the final resting place of the Continental Army and the Revolution.

In these bleak circumstances, Washington again led the way. He assigned soldiers to construct their own barracks, offering prizes for the best huts in each unit. And then he showed them what it meant to endure by camping in his field tent until every soldier had been housed. Throughout the long winter, Washington was constantly with his soldiers, encouraging and training them.

Conditions did improve. The army was fed and clothed. And the men followed Washington's example. They bore their hardships with surprising cheer. They became committed and united as never before.

Nothing teaches better than example. Cyrus McCormick's reaper could harvest a field of wheat more than ten times faster than a man could do it by hand. But farmers were dubious about the benefits of the expensive machines. McCormick convinced skeptics by harvesting field after field himself. Seeing what reapers could do, farmers bought them and revolutionized agriculture.

Experience

Never trouble another for what you can do for yourself.

—THOMAS JEFFERSON

Von Steuben Trains a Professional Army

During the winter at Valley Forge, Washington's army was greatly strengthened by the arrival of Baron Freidrich Wilhelm von Steuben. While most of von Steuben's credentials were fictitious, he was honest about one claim: von Steuben had the best of military experience. He had served on the staff of Frederick the Great, the most advanced military organization in the world. Von Steuben knew how armies worked. He was also a brilliant drillmaster. He had turned the rawest of recruits into competent soldiers.

Von Steuben whipped Washington's army into shape. He created suitable drill and maneuvering procedures. He taught the army to use bayonets, an unfamiliar art that had frightened the Patriots in the past. And although he was an officer, he also acted as drillmaster, cursing his charges in German, French, or whatever language was handy. The army grew proud and confident as they mastered the new skills.

> Revolutionaries often need experienced help. Richard Sears could write copy that sold almost anything. His mail order business grew rapidly from hawking watches to selling surplus products at deep discounts. However, Sears's company remained the number two mail order house behind Montgomery Ward because Sears was a poor manager. That changed in 1895 when Sears hired Julius Rosenwald to run the company. Rosenwald was an excellent manager. With Rosenwald's experience and Sears' promotional copy, Sears increased sales fourteen times by 1900 to surpass Montgomery Ward as the leading mail order company.

Melding

A good example is the best sermon.

—Benjamin Franklin

Creating a National Army

One of Washington's greatest achievements was teaching soldiers from the different states to fight together and to think of each other as Americans. Patriots identified with their states first. They were suspicious of the loyalty and competence of their allies from other states.

Washington was able to break down many of these barriers at Valley Forge. Because the regiments were greatly under full strength, he combined units from different states together for drills. Washington's troops got to know and trust each other as they worked together. They started thinking of themselves as Americans fighting for their nation, instead of as Pennsylvanians or Virginians cooperating with outsiders to win their state's independence. Under Washington's leadership, the Continental Army emerged from Valley Forge confident, united and ready for a fight. It was one of Washington's greatest triumphs. Valley Forge created the army that made the nation.

Modern businesses face a similar problem. They often need to grow through mergers and acquisitions. But merging is more than combining financial statements. People from different cultures must learn to work together. It is always harder than

[113]

you think. One study of mergers in the 1990s found that the revenue growth of merged companies usually slowed. Acquirers had growth rates four percent below industry peers. And more than forty percent actually had total revenue decline. Building a team out of the various parts is as important as taking advantage of the new synergies.

Make Success Essential

We must all hang together, or most assuredly,
we shall all hang separately.

—Benjamin Franklin

The Conway Cabal

After the fall of Philadelphia and Germantown, some Patriots thought General Gates should replace Washington as commander in chief of the army. Washington was losing battles while Gates was given the credit for the victory at Saratoga. And Washington and Congress disagreed on several issues, including the status of Tories and half-pay for officers after the war.

Congress promoted one of Washington's most persistent critics, Thomas Conway, an Irishman who had served in the French army, to major general over many of Washington's supporters and gave him the independent post of inspector general. It caused a divisive political struggle. Washington's friends discredited Conway, who resigned his commission.

As the Conway incident shows, America's Founders didn't always like each other. They were a brilliant, talented group with egos to match. Working together under trying, stressful circumstances, they often got in each other's way. There were quarrels, bad feelings, and bitter words:

> *"He is distrustful, obstinate, excessively vain, and takes no counsel from anyone."*
> —Thomas Jefferson on John Adams
> *"That Washington was not a scholar is certain. That he is too illiterate, unlearned, unread for his station is equally beyond dispute."*
> —John Adams on George Washington
> *"The evil genius of America."*
> —Thomas Jefferson on Alexander Hamilton

Despite these bad feelings, the Founders regularly put their egos aside and cooperated. They had to. They knew they would hang if they failed. So they succeeded together.

Give all your revolutionaries incentives to see your revolution through to the end. During the aborted WorldCom-Sprint merger, Sprint employee stock options vested when the deal was approved by shareholders, rather than when the deal closed. It was perfect for the individuals involved. They could cash out while the stock price was inflated by the merger but before the merger had been finalized and made to work. Many key contributors took advantage of this and bailed out. Not surprisingly, the merger fell apart.

The Dangers of Secrecy

I push myself to laugh about everything
for fear of having to cry about it.

—Pierre Augustin Caron de Beaumarchais,
arms merchant to the Revolution

Roderique Hortalez and Company

The American colonies had depended on Britain to supply their manufactured goods, including guns and powder. The war cut off these vital supplies, threatening to leave Patriot armies defenseless. Dutch and even avaricious English merchants shipped powder and guns through the Dutch colony of St. Eustatius. But much bigger shipments were needed to sustain the war effort.

The American agent in London, Arthur Lee, approached the French about supplying arms. King Louis XVI was interested. A long war between Britain and her American colonies would seriously weaken British power. And if the colonies won independence, it would be even more advantageous for France. Louis was anxious to provide arms to the colonies, but only if France could avoid going to war with Britain.

The French government used its secret agent Pierre Augustin Caron de Beaumarchais to funnel covert assistance to the Americans. Beaumarchais and Lee arranged to have supplies moved through a front organization, Roderique Hortalez and Company. France and its ally Spain each contributed one million livres—a currency formerly used in France, originally worth a pound of silver—to fund the operation. Beaumarchais used the money to buy "surplus" war material from French and Spanish arsenals and ship it to America. Congress sent Silas Deane to France in 1776 to help coordinate the flow of arms. Together, Beaumarchais and Deane supplied many shiploads of desperately needed guns and powder with great discretion.

Beaumarchais was also a brilliant playwright. He wrote the comic plays *The Barber of Seville* and *The Marriage of Figaro,* which were later made into operas by Gioacchino Rossini and Wolfgang Amadeus Mozart, respectively. With his keen sense of humor, he must have appreciated the trouble that the secrecy surrounding his arms operation later caused. Beaumarchais and Deane bought war materials on credit, planning to pay for them with French and Spanish grants and funds Deane had been authorized to spend by Congress. Because of the great secrecy surrounding the operation, they did not carefully document their transactions. When Arthur Lee learned that Deane was paying for supplies that Lee thought were gifts of the French and Spanish governments, Lee and his brother William accused Deane and Beaumarchais of fraud. Deane was recalled from France to give an accounting.

The supporters of Deane and the Lees had a divisive fight in Congress over Deane's accounts. Congress refused to reimburse many of Deane's expenses, and the careers of Deane and the Lees were ruined. Deane returned to France to get documentation to exonerate his actions. While he was there, confidential documents relating to the operation were published that angered both the Americans and the French. Silas Deane fled France and never returned to America. He spent his last years impoverished in England. Congress finally recognized the injustice done to Deane and settled with his heirs in 1842. Silas Deane and Arthur and William Lee were all dedicated Patriots.

Their destructive quarrel was the direct result of the confusion caused by the secrecy of the Hortalez and Company supply operation.

Secrecy is often needed to start a revolution, but abuse or misunderstanding is inevitable without honest disclosure. The inflated earnings at Enron that were hidden by opaque accounting have a long lineage. Chicago grain elevator giant Munn & Scott had a similarly spectacular collapse in 1872 when inspectors discovered it was missing three hundred thousand bushels of grain carried on its books. Wheat prices collapsed and the economy of the nation was damaged because secrecy had been abused.

It Takes Friends

We are all...in agitation, even in our
peaceful country. For in peace as well as in war,
the mind must be kept in motion.

—THOMAS JEFFERSON,
TO THE MARQUIS DE LAFAYETTE, 1823

Benjamin Franklin's Communal Success

On September 26, 1776, Congress appointed Benjamin Franklin to join Silas Deane as American commissioners to France to seek aid for the Revolution. Thomas Jefferson was also appointed but declined because of his wife's poor health and was replaced by Arthur Lee, who was in London. Deane's covert Hortalez and Company supply operation was already underway. Franklin was charged with increasing both covert and overt aid from France.

Franklin slipped across the Atlantic to join Deane and Lee on the sloop *Reprisal* and, evading British warships, landed in France. Although Franklin had doubts about the wisdom of aggressively seeking a foreign alliance, he was the perfect choice for making useful friends. Much of Franklin's personal success had come from good friends. Early in Franklin's Philadelphia career, he organized a club called the Junto. Junto members referred business to each other, accelerating all members' rise to prominence. They helped Franklin organize the library and fire department, and their stimulating discussions made good material for Franklin's almanac.

Even Franklin's famous electrical experiments had many supporters. He got his start experimenting with electricity using supplies, pamphlets, and encouragement sent by his friend Peter Collinson in Britain. The Junto experimented with him. Collinson published Franklin's letters on electricity as a book, *Experiments and Observations on Electricity.* After reading the French translation of the book, Thomas Francois d'Alibard made Franklin an international celebrity by demonstrating that lightning contained electricity a month before Franklin's own experiment with the kite.

Benjamin Franklin was one of history's most prolific revolutionaries because he had brilliant collaborators. Smart help was also key to the Carnegie fortune. Andrew Carnegie attracted the best talent available to his steel empire with lucrative salaries and equity. These brilliant managers, like Charles Schwab, repaid Carnegie's investment many fold.

Be Charming

He that drinks his Cyder alone,
let him catch his Horse alone.

—BENJAMIN FRANKLIN

Benjamin Franklin Seduces France

As one of the American commissioners to France, Benjamin Franklin partied his way to victory in the American Revolution. The colonies needed increased French help to win their war. However, after being beaten in the Seven Years' War, the French were reluctant to risk another conflict with Britain. Franklin won them over with his great charm.

Franklin quickly ingratiated himself into the highest circles of French society. He was invited to fashionable soirees because he was so much fun. The French loved Franklin's carefully cultivated frontier philosopher persona. He had lived in Europe for years, but insisted on wearing a woodsman's fur cap. Franklin became the most popular man in France. His image was everywhere, on snuffboxes, plates, and paintings. Many French families hung a picture of Franklin over their hearths, an advantageous position for any ambassador.

Franklin's charm worked. The American Revolution was far away and risky, but Ben Franklin was a friend. Because of Franklin, both the French aristocracy and the country at large were almost ready to support the American cause by going to war with Britain.

Revolutionary ideas and products are not enough. Someone must also charm key decision-makers. Arthur Pitney invented his postage meter in 1901 to eliminate the theft of stamps. But the United States Post Office showed no interest until he teamed up with Walter Bowes in 1920. Within a year, the charismatic Bowes had won Post Office approval and Pitney Bowes, Inc. sales took off. Charm is essential to your revolution's success.

Closing the Deal

A good lawyer, a bad neighbour.

—Benjamin Franklin

The Franco-American Alliance

When word came that the Americans had captured the British army at Saratoga, the American commissioners pushed hard for France to recognize the United States and provide more open aid. However, Louis XVI was reluctant to ally with America because it meant war with Britain. France could ill afford an expensive war. It was great expenses like the American Alliance that ultimately led to Louis's downfall in the French Revolution.

For a time it appeared that even with the American victory at Saratoga, France would still remain officially neutral. Fortunately, the British came to Benjamin Franklin's aid. British emissaries arrived from London with generous terms for settling the war. Although Franklin and the other Commissioners were not interested in returning to the

British fold, the British counteroffer was perfect for closing the deal with the French. The Americans made it clear that the British offers were tempting, but that they would not settle with Britain if France were to join them.

This war promised to do so much to hurt the British and glorify France that, rather than see it end, Louis agreed to a treaty with the United States. Copies of the treaty were put on a fast ship that raced across the Atlantic. The British offer was received by Congress first, but was quickly forgotten when the French treaty arrived. Congress ratified the French treaty on May 4, 1778. France was in the war.

Alternatives must be clear to close deals. While saving Wall Street during the panic of 1907, J.P. Morgan had trouble getting the trust companies at the center of the crisis to cooperate. None were willing to join a collective defense against runs by depositors. The key to the crisis was keeping the brokerage of Moore & Schley solvent. Morgan could save the brokerage, but he made it clear to the trust companies that he wouldn't act to save Moore & Schley until the trusts agreed to cooperate. The trusts reluctantly agreed because the alternative was too terrifying. The panic ended the next day.

Bad Deals

Beware of little expenses.
A small leak will sink a great ship.

—Benjamin Franklin

Recruiting Help for the Revolution

In addition to securing guns and powder for the Revolution, Silas Deane also enlisted a small army of would-be generals to join the Continental Army. Skilled officers, frauds, and adventurers from all over Europe came to Deane offering their services. Deane found it easy to enlist them all by liberally promising high commissions. He was certain that his recruits would be a great boon to the Revolution, although he knew there weren't commands for all the generals he sent.

Deane failed to appreciate how much his bad deals cost the Continental Army and Congress. Patriot leaders were deluged with men carrying letters from Deane demanding commissions as generals, money for their travel expenses, and fat salaries. Getting rid of the horde of supplicants was time-consuming and expensive. And Deane's many bad deals made it hard for Patriot leaders to recognize the valuable volunteers who came their way, like the Marquis de Lafayette or Baron Johann DeKalb.

> It is easy to make a sale if the price is wrong. DuPont sold enough of its leather substitute Corfam to make hundreds of millions of shoes. It was well on its way to revolutionizing the shoe industry. Unfortunately, all those sales were below cost. Corfam was not competitive without a subsidy. Despite its impressive market penetration, Corfam had to be dropped.

De-escalation

Proving that I am right would be admitting that I could be wrong.

—Pierre Augustin Caron de Beaumarchais

Benjamin Franklin

Arthur Lee's attacks over the Hortalez and Company operation were not confined to Silas Deane. Lee also accused Benjamin Franklin of letting Deane get away with fraud. Both Deane and Franklin lived lavishly in Paris, and neither was well-organized or kept adequate records. Lee assumed that Franklin was almost as guilty as Deane and harassed Franklin with accusations.

However, Franklin was wise enough to ignore Lee's provocation. He understood that getting caught up in a bitter fight would only damage the Revolution. He finally answered a belligerent Lee:

> *It is true that I have omitted answering some of your letters, particularly your angry ones in which you, with very magisterial airs, schooled and documented me, as if I had been one of your domestics. I saw in the strongest light the importance of our living in decent civility towards each other, while our great affairs were depending here. I saw your jealous, suspicious, malignant and quarrelsome temper, which was daily manifesting itself toward Mr. Deane and almost every other person you had any concern with. I, therefore, passed your affronts in silence, did*

not answer them, but burnt your angry letters, and received you, when I next saw you, with the same civility as if you had never written them.

Acrimonious fights hurt all involved. Sewing machine pioneers Elias Howe and Isaac Singer were mired in bitter legal battles over patents until a Singer partner, Edward Clark, found a way to de-escalate the conflict. Clark got the major companies to cross-license their patents in exchange for a share of a $15 royalty on all sewing machines. Clark's compromise ended the fighting and made everyone rich.

Holding Leaders Responsible

*No nation is permitted to live in
ignorance with impunity*

—Thomas Jefferson,
Virginia Board of Visitors Minutes, 1821

John Adams Eliminates His Own Post

Congress appointed John Adams to replace Silas Deane in France. When he and his son John Quincy arrived in Paris in 1778, he was not happy with what he found. Benjamin Franklin and Arthur Lee were still feuding over Deane's management of the clandestine Hortalez and Company supply operation. None of the commissioners, including Deane and Franklin, had coordinated their efforts. Each employed multiple agents who also acted independently. The commissioners failed to keep accounts or minutes of their transactions. American affairs were in complete disarray.

Adams wrote to influential friends, recommending that Congress replace the commission with a single minister. Adams argued that the confusion and conflict in Paris could only end when one man was made accountable and responsible. Congress acted on Adams's advice and appointed Franklin its sole minister to France. Adams was out of a job, but he had improved the function of the American mission by creating accountability.

> Because revolutions often sell promises before they deliver results, accountability is crucial to their success. Defense contractor Wedtech Corporation bilked investors and the government out of hundreds of millions of dollars with the help of respectable accounting, investment banking, and law firms. Wedtech's victims relied on the professionals' representations when investing in or contracting with the firm. But the bankers, accountants, and lawyers claimed that Wedtech Corporation's financial manipulations were not their responsibility, although they earned generous fees while knowing of many of the problems. Clear accountability would have helped stop the Wedtech Corporation swindle before so much was lost.

Critical Problems

The Constitution of the United States
is the result of the collected wisdom of our country.

— THOMAS JEFFERSON

The Continental Congress

The same fierce independence that emboldened Americans to rebel against Britain almost proved the Revolution's undoing. Americans were unwilling to be governed by anyone outside their own respective states. There was great distrust between citizens of the various regions. The Mid-Atlantic states thought New Englanders greedy and uncivil. New Englanders despised southerners, who they believed to be haughty and immoral. Rhode Islanders couldn't imagine allowing Pennsylvanians to tax them, and Virginians thought their affairs were none of Massachusetts's business. Being governed by Congress was almost as odious to most Americans as rule by Parliament.

The states gave the Continental Congress very little power to fight the war. Congress was authorized to raise armies, borrow money, and issue currency. But it lacked the power to tax, and that marginalized all its authority. Congress borrowed money for a time, but creditors quickly realized that Congress had no way to raise any money to pay its debts. Loans dried up. The paper money issued to finance the war depreciated until it was worthless. Inflation raged through the states, with devastating effects on the economy and the war effort. Without pay and adequate food or clothing, only Washington's determination kept enough soldiers in the field to thwart a British victory. But as conditions grew worse, even Washington would not be able to keep the army together.

Patriot political leaders understood that unless Congress was given the authority to raise money, the Revolution would collapse. However, they failed to enact the reforms necessary to win the war. Congress was irrelevant for most of the conflict, unable to overcome the differences between the states that crippled the war effort.

The high cost of resolving insurmountable differences is cheap compared with allowing an untenable situation to continue. When the Japanese bubble economy collapsed in 1990, it was clear that painful political and economic reforms were needed to return the nation's economy to full productivity. But since the reforms, including cutting off the credit to failing businesses, would hurt powerful constituencies within the country, Japan instead tried to buy a return to prosperity with low interest rates and massive deficit spending. Just like in the American Revolution, avoiding needed change has only made the situation more desperate.

Patient Financing

In modern wars the longest purse must chiefly determine the event.

—George Washington

Haym Salomon

Haym Salomon was an essential hero of the Revolution. He was one of its most committed financiers. Revolutions are not cheap, and while their returns are often staggering, payoffs are rarely quick. They require patient backers. Haym Salomon loyally supplied the cash that made the American Revolution work.

Haym Salomon started his service to the Revolution as a spy. He secured a position translating British orders into German for the Hessian troops. He passed on all that he learned to Washington. Salomon was perhaps too zealous a patriot, for he did double duty as a saboteur. He was caught and had to flee to Patriot territory.

Salomon turned his considerable skill to financing the revolution. He negotiated and facilitated the French and Dutch subsidies that paid for much of the revolution. He lent a vast fortune to the revolution. He acted as the paymaster for French troops in the Americas, and advanced them money that he was not repaid. He gave money to American statesmen and officials to support them on their missions. He even backed the agents of foreign allies. Salomon was a shrewd businessman and probably knew that he would not be paid back anytime soon. But his support was so complete that he died penniless in 1785.

Revolutionaries need dedicated financial supporters. Milton Hershey got a huge order for his revolutionary caramels made with milk instead of paraffin. To meet the order, the struggling entrepreneur had to borrow money to increase production. But his note came due before the order was complete, and Hershey still needed more money. Frank Brenneman, Hershey's banker, toured the operation and was impressed. Rather than foreclose on Hershey, Brenneman extended the note and loaned Hershey an additional $1,000. Since an extension was against bank policy, the banker put the note in his own name. Because of his banker's faith and patience, Hershey was on his way to great success.

A Clear Purpose

*His precipitate retreat spread
a baneful influence everywhere.*

—JOHN LAURENS,
aide-de-camp TO GEORGE WASHINGTON

Monmouth Courthouse, June 28, 1778

The new British commander, Henry Clinton, feared being trapped in Philadelphia by a French fleet. He decided to abandon Philadelphia for more defensible Manhattan. He sent a portion of his army away by sea while he led the balance in a march across New Jersey.

Washington decided to attack the rear of the British column. The recently exchanged General Lee asked to lead the attack. The Patriots were anxious for a fight. But Lee sent his army forward in great disorder. Uncertain of their objectives and demoralized by Lee's vacillation, the Americans fought poorly. Lee had ordered a retreat when Washington arrived. Washington dressed down Lee, countermanded his orders for a retreat and reformed the Patriot line. Washington gave his men clear objectives and they rallied. The Americans regrouped under fire and gave the British a tough fight.

Night finally ended the battle. The smaller Continental Army prepared to finish the fight the next day. But General Clinton had had enough. He withdrew his forces during the night and quickened his march to safety behind the guns of the Royal Navy. Under Washington's unambiguous leadership, the rout had turned into victory.

People respond to clear objectives. Brewers created a successful new category with light beers. Customers readily understood the advantage—fewer calories—and quickly made light beers a large and profitable segment. But dry beer, a beer with more alcohol, was a disaster. Brews such as Bud Dry and Michelob Dry didn't perform up to expectations. Consumers didn't understand dry beer—do you drink a dry beer because you are not thirsty?—and ignored it.

Self-Control

To persevere in one's duty and be silent
is the best answer to calumny.

—George Washington

Washington's Disciplined Leadership

In battle, George Washington directed the fight with disciplined intensity. His demeanor was critical for his men. His inexperienced officers and soldiers needed a strong emotional anchor to prevent disastrous panic and flight. Washington's calm courage gave his army the confidence to stand up to seasoned professionals. And when things did go wrong, his officers were more concerned with fixing the problem than justifying their actions to an enraged commander.

Washington was not naturally calm. He only mastered his hot temper with great difficulty. But because he was normally so controlled, Washington's select public rages, like his chastisement of Lee at Monmouth, were dramatically effective. At the Battle of Monmouth, his fury was enough to stop his retreating army in its tracks, allowing him to snatch victory from defeat.

In the emotional game of basketball, Phil Jackson has led his teams to numerous NBA championships with Zen-like calm. And, like Washington, staying in control gives Jackson the option of using anger to great effect. The Lakers were trailing late in a playoff game with San Antonio when Jackson picked a fight with referee and was ejected from the game. Jackson's outburst and ejection energized the Lakers, who came from behind to win.

Mastery

I have been your faithful servant so far as it lay within me to be. I have endured.

—George Washington

Fighting in the North Ends

After Monmouth, the British never again mounted a major campaign in the north. They didn't dare. Washington had mastered his command. The Patriots were still outnumbered. They continued to rely on militiamen who came and went as they pleased. But Washington had a core of trained troops that, combined with militia, could beat the British whenever they strayed beyond the protective guns of the Royal Navy. The British gave Washington's new skills the greatest possible compliment. They declined battle with Washington for the rest of the war, choosing instead to only mount invasions far from Washington's army.

Mastery is crucial to long-term success. Anadarko Petroleum Corporation became the largest independent oil and gas company by mastering exploration and production in areas other oil companies wouldn't touch. It patiently pioneered geological analysis techniques that allowed it to find oil in difficult places such as Algeria, dismissed as dry by its competitors. And it used its expertise to extract oil and gas from fields believed too difficult to tap, such as Bossier in East Texas. Mastery completely changes competition by establishing superior abilities that rivals can't match.

Keeping Ambitious Subordinates

*Few men have the virtue to withstand
the highest bidder.*

—George Washington

Benedict Arnold's Treason

One officer that Washington groomed for greater responsibility was Benedict Arnold. Arnold was one of the bravest, most effective officers in the Continental Army. He secured the vital Lake Champlain route to Canada and led a daring march through the wilderness of Maine to attack Quebec. His aggressiveness during the pivotal fighting leading up to Saratoga was key to the American victory. Of the many Americans who switched sides in the conflict, Arnold was the most vilified because he had been one of the rebellion's most courageous and effective combat officers.

Benedict Arnold turned traitor in part because he was frustrated at the lack of recognition given him. His zeal for action made him many powerful enemies. Still, with Washington's support, Arnold advanced and was offered important commands in the army. But Arnold became so frustrated that his avarice and vanity overcame his patriotism.

As military governor of Philadelphia, Arnold met and eventually married a beautiful young Loyalist, Peggy Shippen, who moved in the most lavish social circles. Arnold corruptly profited from his post to support a complementary lifestyle. Charged with misconduct, Arnold was forced to resign as Governor. Incensed, Arnold negotiated his treason through one of Shippen's former British admirers, Major John Andre. Arnold convinced Washington to give him command of the vital Hudson River fortress of West Point, then prepared to betray it for money and a Major General's commission in the British army. Fortunately, Andre was captured and the plot discovered just before the British attack. Arnold escaped. For the rest of the war, he employed his considerable energy fighting for the British.

Arnold's defection wasn't a serious blow to the revolution. Anger at his treachery increased support for the Patriot cause. However, a number of the best leaders in the Continental Army also left the service out of frustration over their lack of advancement, although they remained loyal to the revolution. John Stark and Daniel Morgan were also courageous combat leaders. When promotions went to lesser men with better political connections, they returned home. The cause was hurt by their absence.

Ambitious, effective leaders are often frustrated and tempted to leave. As there is no stigma connected to switching sides in corporate battles, supporting them is crucial. David Sarnoff was one of the key managers in the early RCA organization. His experience was invaluable in several key areas of the business. But because of his ambition and his colleagues' anti-Semitism, Sarnoff's advancement was blocked. Sarnoff was considering going to another company. Fortunately for RCA, he first went to RCA chairman Owen Young. Young recognized Sarnoff's value to the organization and ended the harassment. Sarnoff went on to lead RCA to the pinnacle of corporate glory and success.

Pragmatic Partners

*The cement of this union is the heart-blood
of every American.*

—THOMAS JEFFERSON

Partnership and Marriage in America

Early America may be celebrated as the land of rugged individuals, but those rugged individuals went out of their way to make certain they had a marriage partner. Marriage was essential to most Americans. At least two adults were needed to keep a family functioning. It was also common for a spouse to die early with the survivor scrambling to remarry as quickly as possible. Future widows and widowers often began arranging their next marriage before their current spouse was dead.

Benjamin Franklin, George Washington, Thomas Jefferson, and James Madison all married widows. Benjamin Franklin also had a platonic surrogate wife and family in England to keep him company during the many long years he was in Europe on business.

Necessity made Americans pragmatic about love, courtship, and marriage. In New England, courtships were accelerated by the practice of tarrying. The suitor spent the night with his lady, both supposedly wearing at least their undergarments. If each was still agreeable to the match in the morning, they were quickly married.

Revolutionaries must often be pragmatic about their partners. When Anita Roddick was looking for manufacturers for her Body Shop line of nature-inspired skin and hair care products, her first choice in partners, large contract manufacturers, weren't interested. Roddick didn't wait for them to change their minds. She contracted with a small lab without the volume experience, but that was eager for business, and got her products on the shelf.

Recognizing Opportunity

*The daily advance of science will enable
[the existing generation] to administer the
commonwealth with increased wisdom.*

—Thomas Jefferson,
to the Marquis de Lafayette, 1823

George Washington's Private Life

Amid the unrelenting work of keeping his army and the revolution
alive, George Washington thought constantly of his home. He loved
his estate at Mount Vernon. It was more than a comfortable refuge for
him. Home was also the center of his personal dreams.

Washington had a passion for progress. Seeing that cultivating
tobacco was exhausting the once rich soil of his estates, he searched
for new ways to make a living from his land. He experimented with
imported seeds, crop rotation, and erosion control. He kept detailed
records of his experiments and production on his estates. He loved
reading the latest agricultural journals from England and corre-
sponded with agricultural scientists. He took an avid interest in breeding improved farm animals. He was thrilled when the king of Spain
sent him a rare jackass for his breeding program.

Mount Vernon and the nearby Potomac River were also central to
Washington's other favorite opportunity, developing the American
interior. Washington started his career surveying the wilderness for
land speculators and acquired huge tracts himself. To develop these

tracts, he dreamed of taming the Potomac River with a series of locks and canals. Cheap water transportation would open the interior to settlement and commerce. Washington was right about canals, although it was the Erie Canal in New York that opened the west. But whenever he wasn't serving his country, he enthusiastically pushed forward his own visionary canal company.

For Washington, the joys and prospects of home were much more compelling than the glories of a general or statesman. He served faithfully whenever his country needed him, but he was never seduced by power because there were always more exciting opportunities at home.

There are truly prospects everywhere. Paul Orfalea realized the unobtrusive copy machine he saw in a university library was a huge opportunity. Students and businesses would always need copies. Orfalea rented a tiny garage near campus and began making discount copies. There wasn't enough room in the garage for both customers and the copy machine, but the business was quickly profitable. Orfalea repeated the success with his chain of Kinko's copy stores, all taking advantage of a simple opportunity.

CHAPTER EIGHT

Strategies for Revolution

Unity

*Error of opinion may be tolerated where reason
is left free to combat it.*

—Thomas Jefferson,
First Inaugural Address, March 4, 1801

Georgia, December 1778

In late 1778, the British shifted their attack to Georgia. Besides their lack of success in northern states, the British had another good reason for this change of strategy. Georgia was in chaos. A bitter feud between state leaders Button Gwinnett and Lachlan McIntosh had deeply divided the state and virtually left it without government. The two men ultimately wounded each other in a duel. Gwinnett died of his wounds and McIntosh fled the state. But the continuing conflict between their factions left the state unprepared for the British invasion.

Lieutenant Colonel Archibald Campbell landed 3,500 British soldiers below Savannah at Girardeau's Plantation. Because of Patriot disarray, only one thousand men opposed them. Savannah fell quickly. Another British force under General Augustine Prevost advanced north from St. Augustine and besieged Fort Morris at Sunbury. With no hope of relief, the Americans capitulated. In only three weeks, the British had completely routed the disorganized Patriots and gained control of the Georgia coastline, with only minimal losses. American infighting had enabled a stunning British victory.

Revolutionaries can't always agree, but they must stay united. John and Horace Dodge became two of the wealthiest automobile industrialists through unity. Their trust and cooperation built one of Detroit's largest machine shops. Henry Ford came to them with a huge parts order for his Model A automobile. The brothers stayed together when Ford couldn't pay. Instead, they took ten percent of Ford's company and fought to keep their own business solvent. The Dodges' gamble on Ford soon made them wealthy. They produced their own automobile in 1914 and became auto barons themselves, successful because they were united.

Cover Weaknesses

*Idleness and pride tax with a heavier hand
than kings and parliaments.*

—BENJAMIN FRANKLIN

The British Take Savannah, December 29, 1778

The Americans didn't just lose Savannah. Their army was destroyed because they failed to protect a glaring weakness in their defense. The Patriots wanted the British to make a frontal attack. They hoped to inflict heavy casualties as the British advanced across open ground toward the rebel line. The American position was anchored on either side by swamps. One of the swamps had a trail through it the Patriots knew about. However, they believed the British would never find the trail and left it undefended. The British did learn of the trail from an informer. A detachment of Scottish Highlanders and Loyalists from New York made their way through the swamp, flanked the American army and completely routed it. Ignoring the weakness in the position was catastrophic for the Patriot cause.

Never ignore your position's weakness. Bristol-Myers' launch of Datril couldn't go wrong. It offered all the benefits of the popular pain reliever Tylenol at a much lower price. It was sure to be a hit. But Bristol-Myers forgot that Johnson & Johnson could easily lower Tylenol's price, which they did. The impact of Datril's launch was blunted, and it never gained traction in the market.

Cutting Corners

Lost time is never found again.

—Benjamin Franklin

The Siege of Savannah, September–October 1779

After taking Savannah, the British struck at Augusta and then Charleston but were finally driven back to Savannah by the Patriots. On September 8, a French fleet under Charles Henri Jean-Baptiste, Comte d'Estaing, anchored off Savannah. General Benjamin Lincoln's Patriot army joined him. Together, the allies laid siege to the city. It was the opportunity the French-American alliance had been looking for. The French Navy and a superior Franco-American army had trapped a British army. A victory at Savannah could have ended the war, just like the battle at Yorktown did two years later.

D'Estaing demanded the British surrender. General Prevost, the British commander, asked for twenty-four hours to decide. The delay was magnanimously granted. During the delay, a British unit from Port Royal was able to slip into the city and reinforce the defenders while work on defenses continued. At the end of the twenty-four hours, Prevost declined to surrender.

After delaying when they should have been decisive, the allies became impatient. The British could only be safely attacked by laboriously digging trenches ever closer to their lines. The effort would take days. Comte d'Estaing was not a patient man. As senior commander, he decided on a surprise attack against the formidable British fortifications to accelerate victory.

The Allied attack was set for just before dawn on October 9, 1779. The attack was organized on the left of the allied line where a swamp provided added cover. Comte d'Estaing and General Lincoln led more than four thousand allied troops in the main assault on the left. Surprise was crucial because of the strength of the British fortifications. But it is impossible to keep a secret when thousands of conspirators are involved. A spy betrayed the plan. The British were ready for the assault. The attack swept forward into volleys of musket and grapeshot.

They reached the ditch protecting the defenses, but could go no farther. The allies made a heroic effort, but it was in vain. The British slaughtered more than one thousand members of the allied army.

Entrenched problems yield to meticulous execution, not cutting corners. Colonel Jacob Schick solved an age-old problem because he was patient. While recuperating from an injury in a frigid Alaskan hunting camp, Schick conceived of a dry shaving system that would work when it was too cold to shave with water. After he got out of the woods and the army, he developed his idea. It took years. Schick had to create a small but powerful electric motor and perfect a method to cut whiskers but spare the face. But Schick refused to go to market until the product was ready. His patience was rewarded. When he finally began selling his expensive electric razors, the demand was tremendous, even in the middle of the Depression.

Controlling the Weather

Therefore it is necessary for a man to be fortunate as well as wise and just.

—Nathanael Greene, Patriot general,
in a letter to Alexander Hamilton,
January 10, 1781

The End of the Siege of Savannah, October 1779

After the defeat at Savannah, the Comte d'Estaing became cautious. Sensing a storm, he set out to sea with his army. His fleet was vulnerable to damage from severe fall storms because they were so close to land. Although victory in North America was within the allies' grasp, d'Estaing could not risk losing his fleet. For the French, fighting in North America was a diversion. D'Estaing's main objective was Caribbean sugar. The eighteenth-century sugar trade was incredibly lucrative. European nations prized sugar islands more highly than huge tracts of unprofitable North American wilderness.

When d'Estaing believed a storm threatened at Savannah, he ordered his fleet to sea to avoid it, postponing victory to assure that the sugar revenue would continue to flow. The Comte's prescient action saved his ships. They just escaped a monster storm. The fleet was scattered but not destroyed. But there would be no second chance at Savannah.

It was not the first or the last time weather would change the outcome of the war. Bad weather wrecked offensives and gave cover to surprise attacks. Fleets were stuck in port for weeks waiting for favorable winds. Storms turned primitive roads into impassable quagmires. Much was simply beyond the control of either side during the revolution. But just as d'Estaing's weather sense saved his fleet from ruin, modern revolutionaries can mitigate the effects of external forces by carefully analyzing and hedging against trends beyond their control.

One of the most volatile commodities is cocoa, the key ingredient in chocolate. There are no synthetic substitutes for cocoa. It must be grown in tropical climates near the equator. Weather, pests, and civil war constantly interrupt supplies and prices. Candy giant Mars, Incorporated maintains a staff of scientists and mathematicians to give it the best possible forecasts of cocoa harvests around the world. Using satellite images, economic data, and political reports, Mars analysts create sophisticated models that they use to hedge cocoa positions. They are so successful that some years Mars makes more money from cocoa futures than it does from manufacturing chocolate. No one can control the weather, but it is possible to mitigate its effects.

Cutting Losses

Who has deceiv'd thee so oft as thyself?

—BENJAMIN FRANKLIN

Charleston, April–May 1780

With Savannah and the Georgia coast under British control, General Clinton organized another attack on Charleston. Clinton had learned much from his first failed invasion. This time, he landed fourteen thousand troops safely away from Patriot defenders and enveloped the city. Then he waited for a favorable breeze that swept his fleet past the city's forts with little damage.

General Lincoln should have escaped with his five thousand Continental and militia soldiers. But Patriot leaders convinced him that if Charleston fell, South Carolina would follow. So Lincoln stubbornly maintained his doomed position until Clinton cut off all escape. Too late, the Patriots saw the futility of their position. They surrendered after only a few weeks of half-hearted resistance.

The Patriots lost an irreplaceable army, ships, and supplies, and their sacrifice did nothing to protect South Carolina. The British brutally pillaged the countryside, fostering long-term hatred but neutralizing the south.

Timely retreat can keep small setbacks from becoming disasters. Charles Merrill pioneered selling securities to the masses in 1914. His friend Edmund Lynch joined him in 1916. They built a profitable business selling hot new chain store stocks, such as Safeway, JC Penney and SS Kresge. In 1928, Merrill became worried about the stock market. Brokers don't like to withdraw from a market any more than generals like to retreat, but Merrill sold much of his own portfolio and advised his customers to do the same. His courage saved Merrill Lynch, and many of their customers, from the crash of 1929. Sometimes retreat is the bravest strategy.

Relative Advantages

But as for this damned old fox,
the devil himself could not catch him.

—BANASTRE TARLETON,
LOYALIST COMMANDER

Francis Marion, the Swamp Fox

While the British occupied most of the south, large-scale Patriot resistance was impossible. However, a few brazen guerilla bands continued to fight back. They turned small size into an advantage. Led by Frances Marion, Thomas Sumter, and others, they hit British and Loyalist units and garrisons and then disappeared into the swamps.

Marion was particularly audacious. General Cornwallis, who took over from Clinton, became so frustrated at Marion's success that he sent Banastre Tarleton to run him down. Tarleton led one of the most feared Loyalist units, the Loyal Legion. "Tarleton's Quarter," the practice of slaughtering surrendering soldiers, was named for him after he massacred hundreds of Virginians at Waxhaw. His hard-riding men had caught and mauled a number of tough Patriot units. But young Tarleton met his match in Francis Marion, a man old enough to be his father.

Tarleton searched for days for the elusive Marion. Whenever he got close, Marion gave him the slip in impassable swamps. Tarleton was finally recalled. The swamp fox was too much for him. Marion continued to be a powerful force in the south, keeping alive the revolution despite the pervasive British occupation. As Nathanael Greene later wrote in praise of Marion:

> *Surrounded on every side with a superior force, hunted from every quarter with veteran troops, you have found means to elude all their attempts, and keep alive the expiring hopes of an oppressed militia....*

Small size can be a relative advantage. Boddington Group was a small U.K. brewer struggling against bigger competitors. Rather than continuing to compete with its better-financed rivals, it sold its brewery operations. Boddington then focused on the area of its business that small companies can excel in, managing pubs. It quickly grew a profitable collection of pubs, resorts, restaurants, and health clubs.

Attention to Detail

A little neglect may breed mischief.

—BENJAMIN FRANKLIN

Camden, August 16, 1780

After Lincoln's surrender at Charleston, Americans raised a new army to protect North Carolina and drive the British out of the south. Washington wanted to send Nathanael Greene to command the force, but instead Congress sent General Horatio Gates. Gates had been lucky at Saratoga. General Schuyler and other officers set in motion the events that led to the defeat of the British there. Congress impatiently replaced Schuyler with Gates just before the trap closed and made Gates a hero. After Saratoga, Gates believed he should replace Washington as commander in chief. He planned to show this superiority by winning another quick, decisive victory in the south.

Soon after joining his army, Gates ordered it south toward Camden, where the British were gathering supplies. Subordinates pointed out that the army wasn't ready and that there were no provisions along the route Gates selected. But Gates had no use for inconvenient details and proceeded anyway. The Patriot Army arrived at Camden disorganized and hungry. The British had time to prepare for an assault while the Americans reorganized. Then Gates initiated a poorly planned attack that quickly fell apart. Terrified, he fled without even ordering his army to retreat. The American army was slaughtered as it ran.

Leaders pay attention to details. Charismatic William Agee became CEO of Boise-based construction company Morrison Knudsen in 1988. He immediately started the firm on a bold new initiative, building railcars. Agee managed the venture remotely from the comfort of his mansion in Pebble Beach. But the details of the project were too complex for hands-off management. Costs surged. Morrison Knudsen was soon losing a million dollars on every car it built. Agee was forced out in 1995 as Morrison Knudsen teetered on the brink of collapse.

Creating Your Own Luck

I'm a great believer in luck, and I find the harder I work, the more I have of it.

—Thomas Jefferson

Kings Mountain, October 7, 1780

Americans had trouble building European-style armies where the soldiers marched and fired in ranks. American frontiersmen were particularly unsuited to this type of fighting. They were expert at using Pennsylvania rifles, and were often called riflemen. The long, deadly rifles had several times the range of traditional muskets. But rifles took longer to load. Massed and at close quarters, European-style, riflemen were vulnerable to the clumsiest musket fire. Riflemen sensibly wanted to snipe at the British from cover and at a distance. They resisted mass military maneuver, preferring to skirmish. Worse, their rebellious natures made them insubordinate when confined to military encampments. American generals were often happier without the undisciplined frontiersmen.

But riflemen became a great strength to the revolution. They were the finest irregular troops in the world. They could live off the land and outmarch any army in the world. Aggressive and independent by nature, riflemen were expert guerilla fighters. Moving fast, striking hard, and fading into the forests, American riflemen helped turn the tide in the south after the American defeat at Camden.

Colonels Isaac Shelby and William Campbell gathered a force of frontiersmen to pursue a marauding battalion of British and Tories commanded by Major Patrick Ferguson. But when they caught him, Ferguson was ready for them atop a steep hill called King Mountain. The Patriots believed they were outnumbered and Ferguson had a well-deserved reputation for skillful fighting. The situation appeared hopeless, but the rebels found a way to create their own luck.

King Mountain was heavily wooded. The Patriots advanced, using the trees as cover. The British could only shoot back by exposing themselves. When they did, the crack Patriot marksmen picked them off. The Patriots reached the top of the hill and decimated the defenders, who surrendered after Ferguson was killed.

Revolutionaries regularly create their own luck. When Hewlett-Packard introduced ink-jet printers, they were too expensive. Customers preferred cheap impact printers or higher quality laser printers. However, HP rearranged the competitive rules in 1990 by using ink-jet technology to pioneer a color printer for under one thousand dollars. Ink-jet sales soared, driving costs down until ink-jets were both highly profitable and dominating the low-end printer market.

Buying Time

We fight, get beat, rise, and fight again.

—NATHANAEL GREENE, PATRIOT GENERAL,
IN A LETTER WRITTEN AFTER THE BATTLE OF HOBKIRK'S HILL
TO CHEVALIER DE LA LUZERNE,
FRENCH AMBASSADOR TO THE UNITED STATES

Nathanael Greene Turns around the Southern Department

General Nathanael Greene was given command of the southern army soon after Gates's defeat. He didn't have enough men to hold back the British, but he was able to appropriate horses. Mounting his best troops, Greene sent two brilliant officers, Daniel Morgan and Henry Lee, on lightning raids against the British. Morgan had retired from the war. A tough veteran who had led riflemen at Quebec and Saratoga, he had resigned his commission out of frustration over losing key promotions to less-able men. Greene convinced Morgan to rejoin the army. Lee, the father of Robert E. Lee, would earn the nickname "Light Horse" for his skillful handling of Patriot cavalry. Morgan and Lee bought the Patriot army invaluable time to rebuild.

Confident of Greene's decisive actions, the remains of the army held together. Greene appointed a competent quartermaster to feed and arm his army. He pleaded endlessly with local leaders for money, men, and supplies. It was exhausting, unending work. Communities were reluctant to send their militias, fearing local raids by the British and Tory partisans. And fighting and pillaging had stripped many areas of supplies. But state leaders and citizens responded to Greene's energy. He recruited fresh troops and forged them into an army. Under his competent leadership, the Southern Department rose again.

Revolutionaries often must buy time to rebuild after setbacks. When Steve Miller took over Morrison Knudsen in 1995 after its disastrous foray into railroad cars, the company had a ten-day supply of cash. With honesty and shrewd negotiating skills, he won enough time from creditors to begin rebuilding. Miller then refocused the business on its core strengths and stanched the red ink. Finally, he was able to swap the company's debt for new equity. Morrison Knudsen emerged a much smaller company, but it was back in business.

Know Your Competition, Know Yourself

Colonel Tarleton is said to be on his way to pay you a visit. I doubt not but he will have a decent reception and proper dismission.

—Nathanael Greene, Patriot general,
to Daniel Morgan

Cowpens, January 17, 1781

One of General Daniel Morgan's detachments mauled a Tory raiding party at Hammond's Store, South Carolina. Hearing of the defeat, Loyalists abandoned another outpost, Fort William. Cornwallis found his position unraveling. With Morgan and Lee at large, he could not gather loyal troops and supplies to hold captured territory. The Patriot raiders had to be stopped.

Cornwallis transferred some of his troops to Banastre Tarleton's Loyal Legion and ordered him after Morgan. Morgan learned that Tarleton's force was coming and prepared to meet him at a site called Cowpens.

Cowpens was an unlikely battlefield, violating the basic rules of eighteenth-century warfare. There were no natural obstacles to anchor the Patriot flanks, just open ground. Tarleton could easily go around Patriot lines. The Broad River behind the Americans prevented retreat. But Morgan understood exactly what he was doing. Tarleton always attacked head-on. And with retreat impossible, the Patriots would have to stand and fight.

Morgan positioned his army to get the most from each man. He placed two ranks of militia in front of his veteran Continental troops, knowing the raw militiamen would run. Morgan even ordered the militia to retreat after they fired a few rounds. The river and the open ground prevented them from going far. While the Continentals stopped Tarleton's weakened attack, Morgan could rally the militia.

The battle unfolded as Morgan had planned. Tarleton went straight for the militia, who picked off many of the British officers before retiring. The Continentals stopped the British advance with withering volleys. Then they drove forward with bayonets. Some of the militia returned to the fight with the Patriot cavalry and the British attack crumpled. The defeat broke the effectiveness of the Loyal Legion and further isolated the British in the south.

Understanding your own capabilities and those of the competition can lead to daring decisions. Nissan closed its flagship Murayama auto plant while pushing ahead with plans to expand existing American production and build a new plant in Canton, Mississippi. Nissan realized that the locus of its competition was shifting to North America. They needed dollar-based costs and plants close to their customers if they were to remain competitive. Aligning strategy with the realities of the competitive situation works, even if it breaks with tradition.

The Right Time

To be prepared for war is one of the most effectual means of preserving peace.

— GEORGE WASHINGTON,
FIRST ANNUAL ADDRESS TO BOTH HOUSES OF CONGRESS,
JANUARY 8, 1790

Guilford Courthouse, March 15, 1781

After the Patriot victory at Cowpens, Cornwallis was determined to destroy General Greene's Patriot army at all costs. Cornwallis burned most of his own baggage and wagons and, with his leaner army, pursued Greene. Greene wisely ran. In a brilliant retreat of more than two hundred miles, Greene eluded Cornwallis and escaped across the Dan River into Virginia just ahead of the British. The Patriots refused to fight until the time was right.

Greene continued to build his army in Virginia until he felt strong enough to challenge Cornwallis. He then met the British on ground of his choosing, at Guilford Court House, North Carolina. Greene mauled the British before he was forced to retreat. Much of his militia had run, denying Greene the victory. But Cornwallis was beaten. He had lost half of his force during the campaign. Soon after the battle, Greene advanced to resume the fight, but Cornwallis chose to declare victory and retreat to the coast and the shelter of British ships.

Greene took advantage of Cornwallis' sudden withdrawal to go on the offensive. He headed south, retaking British garrisons. The Americans suffered a setback when they were surprised at Hobkirk's Hill in South Carolina, but Greene quickly recovered and continued his advance garrison after garrison. By waiting until the time was right, Greene was about to push the British from the south.

Good timing is everything. Railroad magnate Jim Hill got his start by buying the bankrupt St. Paul & Pacific Railroad during the panic of 1873. The railroads' creditors were frightened by the recession, and gave Hill the railroad for less than seven million dollars. A modest improvement in the economic climate let Hill sell the railroad's land grants for thirteen million dollars, providing the capital to build the line into the Great Northern Railroad, the dominant railroad between Chicago and Seattle.

Recognizing Failure

By oft repeating an untruth,
men come to believe it themselves.

—THOMAS JEFFERSON,
TO JOHN MELISH, 1833

Virginia Invaded, 1781

In 1781, General Clinton sent the newly commissioned British general Benedict Arnold to raid Virginia. General Cornwallis also marched into the state on his own initiative. The British concentrated on Virginia because few other options remained. It was the only place their war strategy hadn't failed.

King George and his ministers had assumed that if they punished the rebellion through force of arms, the colonists would return to the imperial fold. George was partially right. Americans did tire of the revolution. Washington's army shrank to a few thousand hungry men. The economy was in shambles. The colonists were desperate for the war to end.

But the flaws in British strategy were now obvious. Military actions punishing Americans also alienated them. Wherever the British army went, it made Patriots of Americans. And conflict with the American rebels had spread to Europe. Britain was at war with France, Spain, and the Netherlands. Russia, Prussia, Denmark, and Sweden were allied as armed neutrals to curb British power and open the lucrative American trade to their ships. Britain's most valuable colonial possessions from the priceless sugar islands of the Caribbean to the strategically vital fortress of Gibraltar were under attack. As an unintended consequence of the war, the whole empire was at risk.

Invading Virginia did not change the dynamics of the conflict. Defeat was only a matter of time. The British needed to recognize the failure of war and redirect their energies where they could succeed.

Recognizing failed strategies is critical to success. David McConnell's customers seemed to like the perfume he sold door-to-door in the 1880s. But despite good sales, McConnell realized his strategy was failing. His female clientele was uncomfortable with a salesman. So McConnell hired Mrs. P.F.E. Albee, the first saleswoman of what later became the Avon Company, and his business took off.

Focus

Reason, too late perhaps,
may convince you of the folly of misspending time.

—GEORGE WASHINGTON

Eutaw Springs, September 8, 1781

After resting his army through the heat of the summer, Nathanael Greene resumed pursuit of the British in September 1781. He engaged the British detachment of Lieutenant Colonel Alexander Stewart at Eutaw Springs near Charleston after a grueling forced march. The Patriots drove the British from the battlefield in a bitter fight. But as Greene's ragged soldiers surged through the British camp pursuing their beaten foe, they began looting. The food, spirits, and clothing were too much of a temptation for the Americans, many of whom were literally naked and starving. They stopped to grab a shirt or a meal, giving the British a chance to regroup. Stewart's men counterattacked, driving away the almost victorious Americans.

Distractions can defocus even sure winners. Scott Paper developed a paper that could be used as disposable clothing for NASA in the early 1960s. But a 1966 promotion offering a disposable dress for $1.25 turned paper clothing into a huge fad. Hundreds of thousands of disposable items were sold or given away, including Nixon dresses, paper furs, and disposable bikinis. The fad burned itself out quickly. After the distractions of high fashion went away, paper clothing found a very profitable niche as medical scrubs.

Leading Rebels

You say to your soldier, 'do this,' and he doeth it, but here I am obliged to say, 'This is the reason why you ought to do that,' and then he does it.

—FRIEDRICH WILHELM VON STEUBEN, PATRIOT GENERAL

Lafayette Marches to Virginia, 1781

Washington sent Lafayette to stop Benedict Arnold's raiders in Virginia. The young nobleman found the Americans difficult to manage. The same qualities that made Americans excellent rebels also made them difficult to weld into a traditional army. Patriots had no qualms about rebelling against their king. When they felt their rights were in jeopardy, they organized themselves and left their farms and businesses to fight. They braved the royal hangman, cannon fire, winter cold, and starvation for their freedom.

This same spirit made it hard for them to accept the discipline of the Continental Army. Patriot soldiers demanded a good reason for whatever they did. They voted on strategic and tactical decisions. Sometimes they rejected their commander's plan of battle.

Lafayette learned an important lesson about leading revolutionaries during the Virginia campaign. His men were tired of the rigors of war, made worse by their lack of meaningful engagements. Many were deserting. Lafayette told troops that they were setting out on a dangerous expedition. He asked his soldiers not to abandon him but said he allowed any who wanted to leave to do so. No one left, desertions ended, and the army fought well.

Revolutionaries are harder to lead than mercenaries, but they make the best soldiers. Ricardo Semler's Brazil-based Semco S/A conglomerate achieved spectacular growth during difficult economic times by treating its employees like partners. Semco divulges its financial information, including executive salaries, to all employees. Workers divide profit sharing funds, pick plant sites, and many set their own salaries. Semco is still a business, not a big, happy family. But Semler's revolutionary management works. The company grew more than 900 percent in ten years and one of Brazil's tough labor unions has called Semler the only good boss in Brazil.

Critics Don't Win Revolutions

Here, again, some blustering hero,
in fighting his battles over a glass of Madeira,
may take upon him to arraign the conduct of our general, and stigmatize the army as cowards.

—PATRIOT MAJOR SAMUEL SHAW,
IN A LETTER TO FRANCIS SHAW,
SEPTEMBER 30, 1777

Maneuvering in Virginia, 1781

Lafayette's early Virginia campaign was a disaster. A small French fleet failed to dislodge the Royal Navy from Chesapeake Bay. Arnold's British raiders were reinforced and moved up the James River toward Richmond. Cornwallis's army arrived from North Carolina, increasing the British ranks to seven thousand men against Lafayette's one thousand. Virginia's government was paralyzed and did little to resist the invaders. Lafayette could only avoid being caught and crushed.

Critics lambasted the Patriot failures, but their criticism didn't turn the tide in Virginia. Lafayette coordinated a brilliant recovery. His small force feinted, advanced, and retreated, applying continual pressure but never allowing the British to force a decisive battle. When he was reinforced with General Wayne's Pennsylvania troops and local militia, Lafayette went on the offensive. But Cornwallis's combined army had had enough tough campaigning. Rather than meet Lafayette's advance, he withdrew down the James to establish a base at Yorktown. Lafayette's tenacity saved Virginia and set up the decisive battle of the war.

Finding flaws is easy. Making strategies work takes real genius. Herbert Henry Dow was ridiculed for trying to build a business producing chlorine for bleach. Large European chemical companies dominated the market, and producing chlorine was dangerous. Dow ignored the critics. He perfected a safe process for making bleach and continued to produce his product while the European competition cut their prices in half in an unsuccessful attempt to drive him out of business. Dow created a viable American chemical business because he ignored the critics.

Contradictory Ideas

We are to guard against ourselves;
not against ourselves as we are, but as we may be;
for who can now imagine what we may become
under circumstances not now imaginable?

—THOMAS JEFFERSON,
TO JEDIDIAH MORSE, 1822

Jefferson's Paradoxical Genius

Thomas Jefferson was serving as Governor during the British invasion of Virginia. It was a trying time. While British soldiers ravaged the state, Jefferson struggled against legal obstacles that prevented him from organizing resistance. And his beloved wife was sick. But in the midst of all these troubles, Jefferson found time to write an excellent book, *Notes on the State of Virginia*.

Thomas Jefferson was capable of pursuing many ideas simultaneously. His interests ranged from anthropology to natural history to religion. But it was his capacity for contradictory thinking that most frustrates his modern admirers. Jefferson espoused inconsistent ideas with ease. The talent was manifest as blatant hypocrisy, but also as pragmatic genius. Jefferson was later the central critic of a strong Federal power during Washington and Adams's administrations. But when Jefferson became president, he had no qualms about using and strengthening those powers to set the nation on a course of his choosing, particularly his purchase of the Louisiana Territory.

> Contradictory thinking can lead to brilliance. Cornelius Vanderbilt made his first fortune by focusing on how to make his competitors most profitable. Vanderbilt ran brutally competitive steamboat fleets. But he didn't try to put his rivals out of business. He forced them to buy him out. The competitor who bought one of Vanderbilt's lines became a profitable monopolist. He could afford to pay a high price for Vanderbilt's operation, especially since the alternative was bankruptcy. Vanderbilt's contradictory thinking amassed enough money to make him a major player in the next revolution that came along—railroads.

Change Takes Time

God helps them that help themselves.

—Benjamin Franklin,
Poor Richard's Almanack 1736

Smallpox Inoculations

Smallpox was one of the most deadly scourges in eighteenth-century America. It was so destructive to the Continental Army that George Washington began insisting that his new recruits become immune to the disease. Otherwise, they were likely to spend much of their tour of duty sick, draining the meager resources of the army, or dying without ever seeing action. Recruits had to have had the disease or be inoculated before they joined the army.

Smallpox inoculation was only just becoming popular during the war. The procedure had been controversial for years. In 1721, during a Boston epidemic that killed ten percent of the population, Cotton Mather and Dr. Zabdiel Boylston tried the daring treatment to keep Bostonians from dying. They learned it had been used for centuries in Africa and the Middle East. Patients were infected with the disease from the pus of others who were already sick. They became ill, but most recovered. The recovery rate for the inoculated was far higher than for those that contracted the disease naturally.

Still, opposition to inoculation was fierce. Making a patient deathly ill did not seem responsible. Benjamin Franklin's brother James railed against inoculation in his paper. Others resorted to physical violence against those who practiced inoculation.

Benjamin Franklin observed the results of inoculation for many years and was convinced that it worked. He was about to inoculate his son Francis when the boy contracted smallpox naturally and died. Heartbroken, Franklin still published articles showing that inoculation was effective. Years of good publicity and personal success finally began changing minds, and the bitter but effective treatment was accepted.

It takes time to change habits. Thomas Cook pioneered the travel business in 1841, when few people left home. Cook arranged everything so that his customers wouldn't need to personally deal with the traumas of their eleven-mile English Midlands excursion from Leicester to a temperance society meeting in Loughborough. It was a great success. But like all new ideas, it took time and positive experiences for people to appreciate that they could travel for pleasure and dare to roam beyond their hometowns.

Decide with Real Data

Persons of good sense, I have since observed, seldom fall into disputation except lawyers, university men, and men of all sorts that have been bred in Edinburgh.

—BENJAMIN FRANKLIN

Bleeding

Revolutionary-era medical care was almost as dangerous as smallpox. Bleeding was the established medical procedure of the day. George Washington may have been indestructible on the battlefield, but his death was later hastened by his physicians' repeated bleedings.

After becoming seriously ill, the retired president was bled repeatedly by a team of eminent local physicians. We don't know if Washington would have recovered if he had not been bled, but the bleeding did weaken him and certainly killed many others.

Bleeding's wide application and the many people who survived it were accepted as proof that it worked. However, these evidences of bleeding's efficacy left out a crucial piece of data: a valid comparison.

Decisions require data that can be used in a comparison. David Ogilvy became one of history's most successful advertising executives by using data to measure the effectiveness of his advertisements. Few businesses are more dependent on creativity and innovation than advertising. Ogilvy was among the most creative. But by gathering hard data, he also knew just how effective his innovations were, such as that a large initial letter in a paragraph increased the readership of an ad by thirteen percent. Using hard data, Ogilvy built one of the most creative and successful advertising empires.

The Risks of Plain Speaking

Washington got his reputation of being a great man because he kept his mouth shut.

—JOHN ADAMS

John Adams in Paris, 1780

In late 1779, after writing a draft of the Massachusetts constitution, John Adams returned to Europe to negotiate a peace treaty with Britain. However, his mission quickly ran into trouble. While waiting for a chance to open negotiations with Britain, Adams held discussions with Louis's foreign minister, Charles Gravier, Comte de Vergennes. Adams accused Vergennes of negligence in France's support for America. He was correct in discerning that the French did not want a speedy victory. Vergennes would have been happiest with years of bitter fighting. But while France was not a selfless ally, its self-interested support was still key to an American victory. Adams's plain speaking was not well-received, particularly since Vergennes was disappointed by the size of the armies Congress had raised to fight the British. Vergennes soon refused to deal with Adams, and America and France continued the polite fiction of fraternal alliance as they pursued their own ends together.

John Adams proved one of the smartest of all the Founders. He was an expert on governance and laid the intellectual groundwork for the governments that emerged from the revolution. Adams was also selfless in his service to his nation. He endured long, painful years away from his beloved wife, Abigail, who ran the farm to support the family in John's absence. But Adams's habit of saying exactly what he thought limited his influence and the recognition he received. Colleagues thought him outspoken and irascible. Even Adams seemed to recognize how his own outspoken habits were a liability.

Still, he found it impossible to refrain from speaking his mind, although it often caused him trouble. Later, as Washington's vice president, Adams's blunt style isolated him from policy discussions. Even as President, Adams so alienated his own cabinet that they listened to Alexander Hamilton in New York more often than they took orders from Adams.

Plain speaking makes entertaining reading and good history, but discretion is usually wiser. Sun Microsystems's Scott McNealy's frank and witty warnings of Microsoft's growing power in the computer industry made him one of the world's most quoted CEOs. His analysis has consistently proved accurate. But plain speaking has also hurt Sun. Microsoft has blunted or diverted industry adoption of Sun innovations like the Java programming language because Sun is viewed as such an implacable opponent.

CHAPTER NINE

SMALL REVOLUTIONS, BIG CONSEQUENCES

✶ ✶ ✶

Too Successful to Innovate?

What is the use of a new-born child?

—BENJAMIN FRANKLIN

Breech-loading Rifles

The Revolutionary War was fought with muzzle-loading muskets and rifles. Powder and shot had to be rammed from the muzzle to the base of the bore. Reloading was time-consuming and the weapons were useless in wet weather. It wasn't until the nineteenth century that firearms that could be loaded quickly via a breech in the bore became popular.

However, effective breech-loaders were available during the American Revolution. Patrick Ferguson, the British officer killed during the pivotal Patriot victory at King Mountain, gave much to His Majesty's war effort. But what could have been his greatest contribution was ignored. Ferguson invented a practical breech-loading rifle. The gun could be reloaded twice as fast as a musket and was very accurate. It even worked in bad weather.

Fortunately for the Patriot cause, the mighty British army felt it didn't need better guns to win. Although initially encouraging, Ferguson's superiors lost interest in revolutionary weapons. Ferguson's innovation died with him at King's Mountain. Armies would fight with muskets for another eighty years.

Success is no reason to ignore innovation. In the mid-1980s, 80 percent of Western commercial airplanes flew with Pratt & Whitney engines. But dominant Pratt & Whitney failed to innovate as fast as competitors, focusing instead on existing business. In the 1990s, competitors produced better engines and won new orders. Pratt & Whitney's share of new commercial engine sales dropped to 4 percent in 2001.

Patience

To err is human, to repent divine; to persist devilish.

—BENJAMIN FRANKLIN

The *Turtle*, September 6, 1776

Connecticut native David Bushnell conceived of a craft that could approach blockading British warships undetected, attach explosives, and blow a hole below the water line. He built this primitive submarine, the *Turtle*. It was a marvel. Bushnell had pioneered solutions that would be used on twentieth-century submarines. The *Turtle* submerged by letting water into a ballast tank and surfaced by pumping it out. It had a snorkel and a manual propeller. It even boasted a compass and depth gauge.

On September 6, 1776, the *Turtle*, piloted by Ezra Lee, slipped below the *Eagle*, flagship of Admiral Richard Howe, the general's brother. However, Lee was unable to attach his explosives to the *Eagle*'s hull because it was sheathed in metal. He ran out of air and was forced to resurface. Dawn broke before he could get away, but Lee dissuaded pursuit by releasing and detonating his bomb. He escaped and *Turtle* made several more unsuccessful attacks on British warships. However, the swift currents of New York Harbor were too much for it. The *Turtle* disappeared sometime during the disastrous retreat from New York in 1776.

The *Turtle* was never rebuilt or improved. Rather than perfect the concept, Americans abandoned Bushnell's innovation. Instead, they invested large sums on conventional warships that were rarely able to leave port. By 1780, improved submarines could have been effective weapons against the British blockade—if Patriots had been patient with the concept.

Revolutionary innovation takes patience. High-tech companies like Go and Apple spent millions trying to create mass-market handheld computers. When they failed, many assumed the handheld concept was flawed. It just needed more work. The

Palm Pilot effectively addressed the issues responsible for early handheld failures. Since then, handheld computers have become pervasive.

Counterintuitive Strategies

He that speaks ill of the Mare, will buy her.

—BENJAMIN FRANKLIN

Good Strategies Are not Always Obvious

The American economy and war effort were heavily dependent on seagoing transportation. Powder, guns, and uniforms were imported. And it was the only efficient way to move goods or critical supplies within the states. Roads were narrow, rough, and rutted. When it rained, the mud was impassable. It cost more to move freight thirty miles on American roads than to ship goods across the Atlantic.

Congress authorized the creation of a navy to protect American shipping. Since the new navy would be much smaller than the Royal Navy, Robert Morris, secretary of Congress's Marine Committee, had a counterintuitive idea for increasing its effectiveness. Rather than try to neutralize British sea power in American waters, the tiny American navy would attack British shipping around the world. A few American warships could threaten numerous British maritime interests, forcing the British navy to withdraw ships from American waters to protect those targets. Patriots had much to gain by widening the conflict, despite their numerical weakness.

Sometimes the best strategies are counterintuitive. The Extreme Programming model of software development is one such innovative strategy for solving a tough problem. Software is notorious for being late and full of bugs. To speed up the writing of good code, Extreme Programming has software developers work in pairs, instead of the traditional one person writing code alone. Programmers write less code per person. But because a partner is always checking the code, and checking it against specifications, teams write more good code per person. It is not an obvious strategy, but it works.

Greed

I do not mean to exclude altogether the idea of patriotism. I know it exists, and I know it has done much in the present contest. But I will venture to assert, that a great and lasting war can never be supported on this principle alone. It must be aided by a prospect of interest, or some reward.

—GEORGE WASHINGTON,
IN A LETTER TO JOHN BANNISTER,
APRIL 21, 1778

The Patriot Navy

Americans had an active maritime tradition, skilled seamen, and ship-building facilities. However, they only deployed a few naval vessels of the modest number Congress authorized. Americans never built an effective navy during the revolution because all their maritime energies were focused on privateers.

Privateers were pirates chartered by Congress or state governments. They preyed on British shipping and were allowed to keep the proceeds of everything that they captured. Privateer owners, captains, and crews could become rich.

Naval vessels of the era also took prizes. It was one of the more common routes to upward mobility in the eighteenth century. But because Congress was so strapped for funds, American naval warships were only allowed to keep a third of the spoils for captain and crew. The rest went to Congress.

It was an easy choice for American shipbuilders and sailors. Shipyards worked feverishly to outfit privateers. Naval ships languished half-finished for want of workers and materials. Privateers signed up almost all the experienced seamen, and many ambitious farmhands as well. Navy ships rotted in port without crews. Americans put to sea an astounding 1,697 privateers during the revolution. Privateers were the most actively and energetically supported effort of the war because they were the most lucrative.

> Greed inspires amazing exertions. John Patterson, the founder of National Cash Register, turned promising salesmen into superstars by inviting them on all-expenses-paid trips to New York City. The men quickly grew fond of their lavish lifestyle and returned home determined to sell enough to afford luxury themselves.

All Things to All People

There are three faithful friends—an old wife,
an old dog, and ready money.

—BENJAMIN FRANKLIN

Money in America

Money in the American colonies had always been a curious hybrid. Although tied tightly to the British economy, Americans didn't always use British pounds and shillings. The British followed a policy of siphoning money out of the colonies. Americans were to buy British manufactured goods and sell foodstuffs and raw materials in return. Ideally, transactions would take place on a semi-barter arrangement so that money need never change hands. Cash was to remain safely in Britain.

Since British money was scarce, Americans used Spanish eight reale coins, or pieces of eight, which they acquired from Caribbean trade. Americans called them dollars, a corruption of the Dutch word *daalder* for a similar German coin. Americans tried to keep these dollars from being shipped to Britain by giving them an artificially high value, with the various colonies legislating widely differing premiums. But even Spanish dollars were so scarce that many types of coins circulated. Promissory notes, warehouse receipts, and government bills of credit were also used in place of money, denominated in a variety of currencies.

After the revolution began, the monetary confusion only increased as the Continental Congress began issuing paper money. Paul Revere made beautiful printing plates, but with nothing to back the currency, "Continentals" were soon worth less than the cost of issuing them. The states released their own money as well. The American money system was a disaster, with scores of different kinds of money circulating at fluctuating exchange rates.

Robert Morris proposed issuing new money worth 1/1440 of a Spanish dollar. All of the myriad coins in circulation would be some whole multiple of the new money. The proposal solved every currency problem in America by being all things to all people, but was cumbersome.

Thomas Jefferson made a counterproposal for an American dollar with the value of the familiar Spanish dollar. Jefferson's proposal also had a revolutionary twist. Instead of shillings and pence, it was to be divided into ten dimes or one hundred pennies. Jefferson's proposal won out. It wasn't easy to convert Jefferson's dollar into all of the many currencies in circulation, but it was familiar and easy to use. Congress adopted Jefferson's proposal, the basis of the world's dominant monetary system.

It is hard to be all things to all people. Bud Hillerich made superb custom baseball bats for himself, teammates, and local professional players, but every customer wanted his bat tweaked until it was "lucky", making it difficult to turn a profit. Hillerich finally solved his problem by creating the Louisville Slugger brand of bats, with a few models like the *Pete Browning*, named for a leading ball player of the time, that allowed each customer to feel he had his own lucky bat. By avoiding being all things to all people, Hillerich was soon mass-producing lucky bats for contented customers all over the world.

Starting Over

I have learned to hold popular opinion of no value.

—Alexander Hamilton

═══════════════════

John Paul Jones

The American Revolution gave an ambitious sailor accused of murder the chance to start over. As a young merchant captain, John Paul killed a mutinous crew member. Although Paul acted in self-defense, the crew accused him of murder. Paul had refused to pay the crew until they returned to Britain, but if he was jailed, the crew could get their money immediately.

With the help of local authorities, the young captain fled, changed his name, and found success serving the new American navy as John Paul Jones. Even though the name change bothered the proud naval officer, he understood that success was better under a new name than no success at all.

There is no reason to carry the stigma of an earlier failure. In 1911, Charles Flint merged a group of struggling companies, Tabulating Machine Co., Computing Scale Co., and International Time Recording Co., hoping to salvage them. The basic idea behind each company of automating data collection and manipulation was a good one, but their names carried too much baggage. When Thomas J. Watson became manager in 1914, he decided that the new company needed an untainted name. He selected International Business Machines, a good name to grow with.

Be Nimble

I wish to have no connection with any Ship that does not sail fast, for I intend to go in harm's way.

—JOHN PAUL JONES

Providence, John Paul Jones's First Command

John Paul Jones is regarded as the father of the United States Navy because of his remarkable record of carrying the fight at sea to the British. Although he often contended with bigger, more heavily armed British warships, his formula for success was simple. He used speed and maneuverability to win when he could, and ran when he couldn't.

Jones was given command of the sloop *Providence*. He cleared the Delaware capes on August 21, 1776. After capturing a whaling brigantine, he headed south. *Providence* ran into a convoy escorted by the HMS *Solebay*. The larger *Solebay* gave chase, but Jones audaciously cut across the *Solebay*'s bow and was quickly out of range before it could change tacks. Jones took two more prizes, the *Sea Nymph* and the *Favourite*, before heading north. Another British frigate gave chase, but Jones easily eluded it. He then captured a British fishing fleet and several more prizes before sailing for Narragansett Bay. Jones succeeded against the mighty Royal Navy because he was nimble enough to exploit opportunities while avoiding the fights he would lose.

Organizations become nimble by giving their people the ability to make decisions and the confidence to take chances. Hewlett Packard grew from a garage to a Dow Jones company by organizing around agile functional groups. Each had profit and loss responsibility. As a result, HP aggressively entered and dominated scores of highly profitable businesses with the speed of a start-up, selling everything from enterprise computing solutions to printers. Nimble business units became first-to-market leaders in categories that bigger, centralized companies were too slow to attack.

Winning against the Odds

He that would fish, must venture his bait.

—BENJAMIN FRANKLIN

Ranger, John Paul Jones Raids Britain

John Paul Jones sailed from Portsmouth in November 1777 aboard the sloop *Ranger.* After sailing to France with news of the American victory at Saratoga, and delays refitting his ship, he headed for English waters. He captured two merchant ships, the *Dolphin* and the *Lord Chatham* and had a skirmish with the revenue cutter *Hussar.* But Jones wanted to cause a major disruption. He knew that Whitehaven

Harbor in Scotland was filled with ships carrying coal to London and other cities. Many would be aground at low tide. Jones went ashore with two longboats and forty seamen. With a few sailors, he scaled the wall of the south battery defending the harbor and tied up the sentries. Jones and a midshipman then spiked the cannon in the north battery before returning to the beach to burn the fleet.

While Jones was gone, a deserter from his crew roused the town. A crowd gathered as Jones started to set the ships on fire. The raiders were forced to withdraw before they could set the entire fleet ablaze, and the townspeople were able to extinguish the fires as Jones rowed away.

The *Ranger* made one more raid on St. Mary's Isle and then met the HMS *Drake* near the entrance of Belfast Lough. Jones defeated and captured the *Drake*, then spirited his prize out of the heart of British waters.

The damage Jones caused was small, but the panic that ensued was huge. Loyal British taxpayers demanded that the Royal Navy be more vigilant in protecting their property from such reckless pirates as Jones. Much of the British Navy was assigned to catch the daring buccaneer.

John Paul Jones was able to take on the greatest maritime power in its home waters because of a simple principle—strengths can also be weaknesses. Britain had a large navy to protect its vital sea-going trade. But there were so many British merchant ships that even the Royal Navy couldn't protect them all. Raiders like Jones could easily find numerous victims.

Take on tough competitors by using their strengths against them. Mail Boxes Etc. competes with the United States Postal Service's huge system of post offices. Their strategy was to provide postal boxes and mailing services, just like the Postal Service. It would seem like a suicidal plan when competing against a huge, established competitor. But the very size of the postal system gave Mail

Boxes Etc. some advantages. Postal patrons often waited years for a post office box. Mail Boxes Etc. can add boxes or stores without bureaucratic delays. Post offices aren't generally located in expensive, high-traffic areas because they need room for sorting and delivery services. Mail Boxes Etc. could locate in small storefronts at shopping centers, giving them a huge traffic advantage. Although they seem to be in a competition they can't win, Mail Boxes Etc. stores have done very well. At this writing, there are more than four thousand franchises.

Never Give Up

I have not yet begun to fight!

—John Paul Jones

John Paul Jones and the *Serapis*, September 23, 1779

After the *Ranger's* exploits, King Louis XVI of France gave John Paul Jones command of a small squadron. Louis spent as little as possible outfitting the ships. Jones's flagship, the *Bonhomme Richard*, was a ponderous converted East Indiaman with cannon ready for the scrap heap. The crew was recruited from released American prisoners, as well as the streets and prisons, and spoke a score of languages. Jones's squadron was rounded out with the *Alliance*, an American frigate with a French captain, and three French naval vessels, *La Pallas*, *La Vengeance*, and *Le Cerf*. Two French privateers, the *Monsieur* and the *Granville*, also sailed with the squadron from Groix on August 14, 1779.

The squadron took several prizes before trouble started. Jones lost two boats and *Le Cerf*. The captain of the *Alliance* became openly mutinous and refused to obey Jones's orders or even sail with the squadron. Then most of the ships were scattered in a gale. After rejoining the *Vengeance* and *La Pallas*, Jones attempted to hold the wealthy port of Leith for ransom but was thwarted by the weather.

On September 23, 1779, Jones found his opportunity. His squadron encountered more than forty ships of the British Baltic merchant fleet escorted by two warships, the *Serapis* and the *Countess of Scarborough*. Jones engaged the larger *Serapis*. The *Pallas* eventually attacked and captured the *Countess of Scarborough*, while the *Alliance*, which was hovering on the wings of the squadron, and the *Vengeance* avoided the fight.

The *Serapis* was faster and more powerful than the *Bonhomme Richard*. Jones quickly realized that he would lose a battle of maneuver and broadsides. So Jones made several attempts to grapple the *Serapis*, finally succeeding when the two ships' rigging became entangled. Seizing the chance, Jones secured the ships together. Gun crews were just a few feet apart. The *Richard*'s main batteries were quickly silenced. The big cannon exploded when fired while shots from the *Serapis* took out the smaller guns. Then things got worse. The *Alliance*'s captain sailed close, but, instead of helping, treacherously fired a number of broadsides at the *Bonhomme Richard*, hoping to be rid of Jones once and for all.

Pounded by the British and the *Alliance*, Jones was in a desperate fix. Sometime during battle, legend has it that Jones was asked if he had struck his colors and surrendered. Jones is said to have replied, "I have not yet begun to fight!" And he hadn't. Jones still had a fighting crew and French Marines on deck and in the rigging, three small deck guns, and his own unconquerable spirit. While the *Serapis* pounded the *Richard* below deck, Jones and crew succeeded in clearing the British from the rigging and deck of the *Serapis*. Although the *Richard* was so badly damaged that it appeared it would sink at any moment, the British captain lost his nerve first. He struck his colors and surrendered to Jones. The *Bonhomme Richard* sank within two days of the battle, a total wreck.

Heroes never give up. John H. Johnson dreamed of starting a magazine targeted at African-Americans, something that he himself wanted to read. Friends and mentors discouraged him. At the end of the Depression, the environment for starting a magazine was bad in general. Johnson would have to overcome the added obstacles of racism and discrimination.

Johnson refused to give up. He borrowed five hundred dollars to mail an offering to twenty thousand potential customers. Johnson got three thousand subscriptions. He printed five thousand copies of his *Negro Digest*, and was able to get newsstands that hadn't carried African-American periodicals to sell the extra two thousand copies by having friends ask for the magazine. Within eight months, his circulation hit fifty thousand. Johnson broke through countless racial barriers and become a wealthy man because he never gave up.

Plain Speaking Continued

The cat in gloves catches no mice.

—Benjamin Franklin

John Adams in the Netherlands

In 1780, Congress instructed John Adams to leave Paris and travel to the Netherlands to negotiate a badly needed loan. After John Paul Jones brought the captured *Serapis* and his British prisoners to Holland in 1779, relations between the Netherlands and Britain foundered. The British declared war on the Dutch soon after Adams arrived.

The British were anxious to cut off war supplies being shipped to America through the Dutch Caribbean colony of St. Eustatius. They surprised St. Eustatius, plundering the rich island. The Dutch were incensed and saw helping the American Revolution as the easiest way to strike back. However, their decentralized governments could not reach a consensus on how to proceed.

Here Adams's blunt talk proved invaluable to the revolution. His message was simple. The Netherlands was already at war and supporting America was the best way to fight back. Now was the time to secure lucrative trading rights by signing a treaty with the United States. Adams's plain speaking and dogged determination cut through the considerable bureaucratic inertia. Adams secured a timely loan and signed a treaty of friendship and commerce.

There is a time for blunt talk. In the 1870s, petroleum refiners were losing money on every barrel they produced because of cutthroat competition. John D. Rockefeller went to his fiercest rivals with a blunt proposal—consolidate or all would be ruined. Rockefeller's competitors quickly saw the wisdom of the proposal and, swallowing their pride, sold out for a share of Standard Oil.

Relations Matter

Character is much easier kept than recovered.

—THOMAS PAINE

═══════════════════════

The End of the Revolution for John Paul Jones

After his victory over the *Serapis*, Jones was a hero in France and America. Even in Britain, songs of admiration were composed about him. But the *Serapis* was Jones's last fight of the revolution. Political enemies succeeded where the Royal Navy had failed, putting John Paul Jones out of action.

John Paul Jones was a naval genius but an abysmal politician. Despite his gallant nature and genuine concern for his men, he managed to alienate much of the Patriot leadership and his own officers and crews. It was simply not in his nature to compromise. Jones's autocratic behavior was typical of eighteenth-century naval officers, but it didn't work for the rebels he reported to and led. The indomitable spirit that brought Jones glory at sea also kept him from greater triumph. Disgusted subordinates and superiors removed him from the fight. Jones did return to action in the service of Catherine the Great. He led a Russian squadron to victory in the Black Sea before his lack of political skill again cost him his command. He died in Paris in 1792.

Personal and political relationships cannot be ignored. Mexico's Industrias Unidas was awarded the nation's mobile radiotelephony monopoly in the 1950s. The franchise became invaluable in the 1980s with the explosion of cellular telephones. But when Mexican telephone company Telmex asked for a portion of the lucrative franchise, Industrias Unidas agreed. It understood it couldn't win in the long run without maintaining important relations.

Speed

I cannot but repeat my entreaties that you will hasten your operations with all possible dispatch; and that you will disencumber yourself of every article of baggage and stores which is not necessary.

— GEORGE WASHINGTON,
IN A LETTER TO GENERAL JOHN SULLIVAN,
JULY 29, 1778

Fighting on the Frontier

Some of the bitterest fighting during the Revolution occurred along the frontiers of New York and Pennsylvania. British loyalists and their Native American allies attacked frontier settlements, torturing and massacring the inhabitants. The raids had little military value, but the human cost was devastating. General John Sullivan led a massive five thousand-man Patriot army into western New York to stop the assaults. After a small action near Newtown, Sullivan marched through the area largely unopposed. His force was so large and so heavily encumbered that its quarry had fled long before it arrived. Sullivan destroyed the extensive Native American farms and sturdy villages in the area, but was unable to catch the raiders. The attacks continued with greater ferocity.

Patriot Colonel Marinus Willett was finally able to bring a measure of peace to the region with a much smaller force. Willett had only five hundred men, but they were fast. By rotating his small force throughout the territory, Willett found the raiders. He pursued them with a tiny contingent while ordering militia units to follow. With only four hundred of his men, he surprised and defeated eight hundred raiders, ending their attack on New York.

> Speed can overcome size. Sam Walton owned a small chain of Ben Franklin stores when he visited an early Kmart on a trip to Chicago in 1962. He was impressed with the scale, efficiency, and variety of the new discount store concept. When he returned home, he found a site and built his own Kmart-style store that he called Wal-Mart. Many other retailing executives were also inspired by the early Kmart volume discount concept, but none moved as quickly as Walton. Sam Walton became the king of retail while his larger competitors plodded into obsolescence.

Be Audacious

*In War it is often impossible to conform to all
the ceremonies of Law and equal justice.*

—NATHANAEL GREENE,
IN A LETTER TO THOMAS JEFFERSON,
APRIL 28, 1781

George Rogers Clark

Early in the revolution, the British controlled the vast American interior with a series of forts supported by Native American allies. George Rogers Clark captured this huge territory with fewer than two hundred men.

Like a true revolutionary, George Rogers Clark won command of an expeditionary force to the Northwest Territory through tireless personal effort. The tall, charismatic young man approached various Virginia leaders with his scheme to secure the Northwest Territory. Virginia claimed most of the territory, and leaders like Patrick Henry and Thomas Jefferson felt the claim would be strengthened if Virginians drove the British out.

Virginia commissioned Clark as a colonel and authorized to him to raise an army. He hid his real objective from his men, claiming instead that he was going to protect Kentucky. He feared that he would not be able to recruit soldiers if they knew they would have to march hundreds of miles into the wilderness against an enemy many times more numerous. But even with this deception, he was able to raise only two hundred men.

Clark didn't reveal their mission until it was too late to turn back. But as he led his band into the wilderness, his men came to believe they could actually do it. His bold leadership inspired and excited his men. Arriving at the settlement and fort of Kaskaskia in present-day Illinois, they found a way to take the outpost through surprise, bluff, and finally magnanimity. They even won most of the locals over to their side. Capitalizing on their good fortune, the Americans quickly captured the towns of Cahokia, also in Illinois, and Vincennes, now in Indiana, and absorbed the local, mostly French, militias. Through sheer audacity, George Rogers Clark had taken a tiny force deep into hostile territory and then found a way to win.

Revolutionaries must be audacious. Milton Bradley bought one of the first lithograph machines with little idea of what to do with it. Friends suggested that portraits of the president-elect, Abraham Lincoln, would sell well. Bradley prepared a large stock of Lincoln portraits for the president's inauguration. But after Lincoln grew a beard, no one wanted Bradley's clean-shaven lithographs of the new president. Desperate for a product, he talked with the inventor of a board game, "The Checkered Game of Life." Bradley bought the game and quickly sold almost fifty thousand copies. Soon he was a prosperous game manufacturer. By audaciously plunging into lithography, Milton Bradley found a way to make it pay to play.

Maintaining Morale

They really began to think themselves superiour
to other men and that neither Rivers or seasons
could stop their progress.

—George Rogers Clark

Repelling the British at Vincennes

In late 1778, the lieutenant governor of Canada, Henry Hamilton, set out from the British fort in Detroit to annihilate George Rogers Clark's small force and reassert British control in the Northwest Territory. Gathering Native American allies as he went, Hamilton retook Vincennes. And then, because of the difficulty of traveling in winter, he stopped. He sent his Native American allies home with instructions to join him in the spring to capture Kaskaskia and complete the rout of the Americans.

George Rogers Clark realized he could not hope to defeat the large force that Hamilton would raise. His only chance was to beat Hamilton before Hamilton's Native American allies returned in the spring.

Clark and his small force started for Vincennes on February 5, 1779. They marched alternately through deep snow and freezing floodwaters. The men often waded for miles through chest-high water. It was a desperate enterprise, but Clark understood that they would never make it if his men thought their situation were desperate. During the day, Clark and his officers treated the march as a game, running, laughing, and shouting through the water and mud. Clark would dab his face with war paint and then march off into the freezing water with a war whoop and a song. Each evening, Clark assigned a company to provide a feast of wild game, with dancing and celebration. It worked. Clark's men thought they were invincible, just like their leader. Clark's tiny army triumphed over the impassable wilderness and arrived at Vincennes.

Clark attacked, careful to keep the British from discovering the small size of his force. They carried the town and besieged the British in the fort. Through bluff and savagery, Clark convinced Hamilton to surrender. George Rogers Clark had motivated his small army to win against impossible odds.

Henry Endicott and George Johnson used motivation to build a shoe manufacturing empire. Industrialists in the 1890s increased profits by exploiting their workers. Endicott and Johnson grew their business by making their company a great place to work. They treated employees fairly and shared profits. Endicott and Johnson even built company towns with subsidized housing and recreational facilities. Workers were intensely motivated. There were no strikes at the Endicott Johnson Corporation during a period of enormous labor unrest. Customers were motivated too. Many would only buy Endicott Johnson shoes.

CHAPTER TEN

THE ENDGAME

The Necessity of Cooperation

*Two Sovereignties can not co-exist
within the same limits.*

— ALEXANDER HAMILTON

Ratifying the Articles of Confederation

In late 1780, the Continental Army had dwindled to three thousand hungry men. Washington warned that his force would collapse without money for food. Congress was broke, but Patriots knew their desperate financial situation could be improved if the Articles of Confederation were adopted. The Articles were created after the Declaration of Independence to give some structure and legitimacy to the new nation. They gave Congress and the new government little real power, but were superior to the ad hoc arrangements under which the Continental Congress operated. Approving the Articles would increase Congressional legitimacy enough to raise a few more months of provisions for the army.

Congress had endorsed the Articles in 1777. But they were held hostage for more than three years because of a dispute over claims to western lands. Several of the states, including Virginia and Connecticut, had colonial charters that gave them control over huge tracts of interior territory. They would have grown to enormous size and influence if their claims had been realized. The other states were resentful of these claims and refused to approve the Articles of Confederation until western land claims were relinquished. The impasse continued through much of the war until it became clear that Americans would lose everything unless they compromised. The states finally relinquished their land claims and ratified the Articles of Confederation.

Even fierce competitors must recognize when cooperation is necessary. Gottlieb Daimler and Karl Benz were implacable rivals, competing in the marketplace and on the racetrack. But after World War I, neither Daimler nor Benz could sell enough cars to make a profit. Faced with ruin, the rivals reluctantly formed a temporary union. Daimler and Benz found they worked so well together that the partnership became permanent in 1926 when Daimler-Benz AG was created.

Sharing Control for Success

It is absolutely necessary that you should curb that very keen sense of missing nothing.

—ROBERT MORRIS, PATRIOT FINANCIER

Robert Morris Saves the Revolution

In January 1781, after almost six years of fighting, Pennsylvania troops in the Continental Army mutinied because they had nothing to eat. Pennsylvania officials ended the rebellion by allowing most of the mutineers to return home. A few weeks later, the New Jersey troops mutinied. Washington suppressed this rebellion forcefully. But it was clear that the army was about to collapse.

At this desperate time, Congress and Washington called on Robert Morris to save the revolution. Morris was a shrewd businessman, and proud of it. After cornering the wheat trade as a fifteen-year-old apprentice, he had used his financial skills to amass one of the greatest fortunes in the colonies. He became even richer from the British merchant ships his privateers captured. Congress appointed Morris superintendent of finance under the recently ratified Articles of Confederation, and charged him with raising enough money to keep Washington's army in the field.

Morris issued new currency backed by his own resources, creating liquidity in the economy. He created the Bank of North America to act as a central bank and stabilize both public debt and currencies. Foreign loans started flowing again as Morris put the Confederation's finances in order. Enough cash was scraped together to feed what remained of the army. The war could go on for another year. However, Morris could only postpone the financial collapse of the revolution. Congress could not function for long unless the states agreed to cede some of their sovereignty to the national government.

Sometimes revolutions must give up control to succeed. In 1984, Apple Computer, Inc. launched the Macintosh, which at the time was the best personal computer ever. It was generations ahead of PCs based on the Microsoft/Intel architecture and led the way in graphics, audio, and video. It could have swept the world.

However, Apple retained exclusive control over Macintosh to capture all of its lucrative profits. Locked out of the Macintosh revolution, other computer innovators focused their energies on the pervasive Microsoft/Intel architecture. Their innovations, or implementations of Mac innovations, slowed and reversed Apple's market penetration. Although it took competitors years to come close to many of the best Macintosh features, they eventually succeeded.

Macintosh is no longer generations ahead. Apple has remained an innovative revolutionary. But by refusing to share control, Apple sharply limited Macintosh's potential.

Seize the Moment

The way to see by Faith is to shut the eye of Reason.

—BENJAMIN FRANKLIN

The March to Yorktown

The French were an active and powerful ally in the revolution. Besides money and arms, they dispatched fleets and troops to aid the Patriots—but mounting a successful joint military operation proved difficult.

A French fleet with troops under the Comte d'Estaing arrived outside New York Harbor in 1778. D'Estaing just missed the chance to surprise a British fleet, and his ships drew too much water to enter the harbor and engage the British warships there. A joint attack on the British in Newport, Rhode Island, also failed because of poor coordination and bad weather.

D'Estaing returned in 1779 for the disastrous siege of Savannah. In 1780, the Comte de Rochambeau arrived with a powerful army, but the British blockaded them in Newport and no action could be mounted. Washington had to send home much of the army he had gathered for the joint campaign because he could not feed them.

Despite the failures, the allies were ready to try again in 1781. Admiral Francois Joseph Paul de Grasse's French fleet would be briefly available after summer operations in the Caribbean, and Rochambeau's army was still in Newport. Washington hoped to mount a decisive attack on New York that would end the war. But when de Grasse refused to attack New York, Washington feared that the year would be another lost opportunity. However, there was still a chance. De Grasse would sail to Chesapeake Bay. Lafayette and Rochambeau urged Washington to besiege Cornwallis's army at Yorktown while de Grasse controlled the Chesapeake.

A Yorktown campaign was a huge gamble. Cornwallis could easily escape the trap, or Clinton could ravage the northern states while the Washington and Rochambeau armies marched the four hundred miles to Virginia. The long march might destroy the ragged Patriot army. And if de Grasse's fleet was late, the gamble would fail. There were so many ways the plan could go wrong. But it was a chance. Washington decided to seize the moment. He ordered his army south, to Yorktown.

Revolutionaries are not afraid to seize an opportunity. When Richard Reynolds first saw lighter, stronger aluminum foil, he realized it would eventually displace the tin foil he produced.

And he knew aluminum would be critical if Nazi Germany started another war in Europe. Reynolds began investing heavily in aluminum production capacity, although there was little demand for the metal. Aluminum demand exploded during World War II, and because of his foresight, Reynolds's aluminum operations grew rapidly. By seizing the moment, Reynolds built an industrial giant.

Grasping Victory

Discipline is the soul of an army. It makes small numbers formidable, procures success to the weak, and esteem to all.

—GEORGE WASHINGTON
TO HIS OFFICERS IN THE VIRGINIA MILITIA,
IN *Letter of Instructions,* 1759

The Battle of the Capes

Admiral de Grasse's French fleet arrived at Chesapeake Bay on August 30, 1781 while the armies of Washington and Rochambeau were still en route to Yorktown. The British had been warned of de Grasse's objective and sent their own fleet under Admiral Thomas Graves to prevent the French fleet from trapping Cornwallis. Both sides knew the outcome of the war now depended on the control of Chesapeake Bay.

On September 5, Graves's fleet arrived outside Chesapeake Bay. De

Grasse's fleet was at anchor and many of his sailors were ashore, but the French admiral quickly formed his line of battle and closed with the British.

The two armadas engaged in a brutal firefight until nightfall. Then the combatants continued sailing within sight of each other through the night and the next day without exchanging a shot. De Grasse was happy to lead the British away from Chesapeake Bay so that another French fleet from Newport could sail to Yorktown unmolested. But curiously, Admiral Graves didn't attack. He knew that if he did not prevail over the French, Cornwallis and the war were lost. With everything riding on his success or failure, Graves did nothing. He simply paced the French, leaving Cornwallis far behind. During the night of September 8, the French fleet turned around and sailed to the Chesapeake. The British fleet returned to New York, giving up the battle and the war.

It seems inexplicable that Graves and other British leaders acted so timidly during this campaign while Washington was willing to risk everything. But in 1781, it was quite clear to both sides that the British would never reconquer America. The British were militarily dominant, but they had lost. It didn't matter how brilliantly they performed. Americans had decided to be independent. Only an occupation force far more massive than the huge armies and navies already in America could have forced obedience. At the first hint of success for Washington's bold Yorktown gamble, the British began to give up. Graves started the capitulation when he gave up the Chesapeake to de Grasse.

Revolutionaries go for victory, even when the odds are against them. At the end of World War II, Soichiro Honda mounted a pine resin engine on a bicycle. It proved an economical solution to severe Japanese transportation problems. Within a few years, he had a thriving motorcycle business. To increase sales, Honda decided to export to the United States. Harleys and Indians, bikes with a tough-guy image, dominated the American market. Honda changed that with his "You meet the nicest people on a Honda" campaign that revolutionized the motorcycle industry. Honda then successfully entered the even more competitive automobile market because he knew in order to win he needed to take risks.

Revolutionaries Win

Humanity has won its battle.
Liberty now has a country.

—MARQUIS DE LAFAYETTE

Yorktown, 1781

The Continental and French Armies made an impressive forced march from New York to Yorktown. At Washington's request, Robert Morris raised four hundred thousand dollars, using his own credit to give the army a month's pay. It was the only remuneration most soldiers ever received, but Washington feared his army would fall apart on the long march without some reward.

By the time the allies reached Yorktown, de Grasse had driven off Graves's fleet and closed the trap. Washington and Lafayette still had to convince de Grasse to remain in the Chesapeake until the British army surrendered. Yorktown easily could have been another missed opportunity. Lafayette performed one of his greatest services to the Revolution, persuading and flattering de Grasse into staying until the end of the siege.

The allies surrounded Yorktown and began work on the trenches that would allow their artillery to command the garrison. Cornwallis made a desperate attempt to escape to Gloucester, across the York River. But this time the weather was on the American side. A storm thwarted the British escape. With Allied cannon now close enough to decimate the entire garrison, Cornwallis had to surrender.

On October 19, 1781, the British marched out of Yorktown and laid down their arms. The Patriots could hardly believe that they had won. They were dressed in rags. The army would suffer another hungry winter while even their new prisoners still had money to buy food. Congress was so destitute that when a messenger arrived with news of Cornwallis's surrender, there wasn't enough money to pay him. But incredibly, the Patriots were victorious.

Sometimes it is just as hard for modern revolutionaries to visualize themselves winning. But they do win. Wilson Greatbatch overcame technical hurdles, funding shortfalls and liability risks to pioneer his revolutionary implantable pacemaker. Worried about their liability, established medical equipment companies shunned the risky project. Greatbatch had to take the risks himself, including building the first devices in a barn. With great persistence, he got the pacemakers tested first on animals and then people. His determination revolutionized the quality of life for thousands of heart patients.

Less to Lose

Necessity never made a good bargain.

—BENJAMIN FRANKLIN

The Peace Treaty

After Yorktown, even King George realized that the war was over. The American commissioners in Paris (John Adams, John Jay, Benjamin Franklin, and later Henry Laurens) began negotiating a peace treaty to end the conflict.

The commissioners could have negotiated a disaster. Congress instructed them to defer to the wishes of the French. And the British still held key American cities while Congress and the Continental Army were rapidly dissolving. But the commissioners understood that Britain needed peace more than America. King George was desperate to end the war with his European neighbors and the drain on his treasury. Although the American position appeared much worse, they could afford to wait. With this advantage, the commissioners negotiated aggressively, winning favorable boundaries with Canada, fishing rights, and the vast American interior, in addition to a recognition of independence.

In negotiations, it is not size or power that matters as much as who has the most urgent need. Be sure your side has the least to lose. Microsoft didn't own the operating system it supplied for the first IBM PC. But to facilitate selling other software tools to the IBM PC project, Bill Gates found and licensed the DOS operating system from another software company. IBM offered Microsoft its standard terms for the software, including the operating system. Instead, Gates demanded the right to sell the operating system to third parties. IBM could have licensed DOS directly from its owner and cut Microsoft out of the deal. But Gates knew that IBM was in a hurry. Hardware was scheduled to arrive in a few weeks. It would take too long to strike a deal with another supplier. So IBM agreed to Gates' terms. Microsoft now has a larger market capitalization than IBM.

Humanity

Where liberty dwells, there is my country.

—BENJAMIN FRANKLIN

Washington Stops a Coup, March 15, 1783

After Yorktown, the Continental Congress and the states completely abandoned Washington's army. They were ready to send the soldiers home without any compensation for their suffering. Washington's officers and men were furious. They resolved to seize control of the government and force payment of the money they were owed. When Washington refused to lead the army against the civilian authorities, many officers decided to proceed with the coup without him. The revolution faced its most serious crisis.

On March 15, 1783, Washington surprised a meeting of his officers. They had been discussing their mutiny and were visibly angry when Washington tried to dissuade them from seizing power to redress their grievances. But then the General pulled a letter from his pocket. He tried to read it, but could not. He pulled a pair of spectacles from a pocket. The officers were shocked. The dignified Washington had never worn them before his men.

Washington apologized, "Gentlemen, you will permit me to put on my spectacles, for I have not only grown gray but almost blind in the service of my country."

Washington's simple demonstration of his own humanity won his officers over. They listened as Washington warned them that a revolt threatened everything they had fought for. He assured the officers that they were heroes and urged them to see their glorious fight through to the end. Then Washington withdrew. The Patriot officers resolved to remain loyal to Congress and Washington.

People respond to sincere humanity. Sam Walton regularly visited his stores, opening a box of crackers and talking with workers. Employees responded to Walton's intimate human concern with loyalty and devotion that propelled Wal-Mart to the top of American retailing.

nation, angry mobs of debtors shut down courts and sheriff's auctions. In Massachusetts, open warfare flared during Shays's Rebellion, with the state militia fighting friends and neighbors who had taken up arms to prevent the loss of farms and businesses. Americans needed a stable national government to address these problems. But that could only happen if the states gave up some of their control.

Sometimes revolutionaries must give up some of their independence to succeed. Walter Jacobs started renting Model T Fords in Chicago in 1918. The business was successful. But Jacobs realized that with more capital, it would be a greater success. Jacobs sold the business to John Hertz in 1923. With deeper pockets, growth accelerated. Jacobs stayed with the company through a number of owners. When Hertz Rental Car was listed on the New York Stock Exchange in 1954, Walter Jacobs was its first president. The company wasn't his and didn't bear his name, but by giving up control, Walter Jacobs was able to grow the business into the world's largest rental car company.

Getting Bigger

There was never a good war or a bad peace.

—BENJAMIN FRANKLIN,
IN A LETTER TO JOSIAH QUINCY,
SEPTEMBER 11, 1783

CHAPTER ELEVEN

As Revolutions Mature

Ceding Power

When there's no Law, there's no Bread.

—Benjamin Franklin

The Difficulties of Union

The United States struggled to function as a nation under the Articles of Confederation. States were unwilling to give up any sovereignty to Congress, leaving the national government powerless. Some states didn't bother to appoint delegates to Congress. The government was almost too weak to end the war. The peace treaty with Britain technically expired because Congress took too long gathering enough delegates to ratify it.

But there were more serious problems. Local economies lacked enough cash to function. Honest farmers and tradesmen were imprisoned because there was no money to pay taxes or debts. All across the

A New National Government

The Confederation was a complete failure on the international stage. It had no authority to look out for American interests. Like Americans, foreign powers disregarded Congress. Some sent ambassadors to the major states. Others ignored America entirely. The individual states, where real power resided, acted like independent nations. But they were too small to be of consequence. The United States suffered economically and politically.

The British occupied forts in American territory like Detroit. The Confederation was powerless to do anything about it. The British also restricted American trade in the West Indies. When Massachusetts, Rhode Island, and New Hampshire retaliated with their own restrictions, Connecticut undercut the effort by encouraging the British trade to come through her ports. Spain refused to grant the United States shipping rights through its port of New Orleans and schemed to gain control of interior settlements. America had to organize as a big nation to be of consequence in the world.

Even the nimblest revolutionaries must think about getting bigger as markets grow. In the 1800s, almost every American town or even neighborhood had its own brewery. Beer spoiled too quickly to be transported far. So brewers were small and local. Adolphus Busch revolutionized the industry when he created a process for pasteurizing beer, killing the bacteria that spoiled beer and limited its shelf life. Suddenly, Busch and other pasteurization revolutionaries were able to sell beer over wide areas from large, efficient factories with marketing efforts that their smaller competitors could not match.

Presume

*There is only one remedy—to call a convention
of the states.*

—ALEXANDER HAMILTON

Alexander Hamilton and the Constitutional Convention

The Annapolis Convention of 1786 was convened to discuss commercial affairs between the states. It was not an important convention. Some states didn't send delegates, and other delegates didn't show up. Lacking a quorum, the Convention could not transact business and would have ended in obscure failure.

However, Alexander Hamilton presumed to use the Annapolis Convention for something it had no business doing. He presented a resolution calling for a convention to reform the central government. The Annapolis Convention had no mandate to call for a Constitutional Convention. It couldn't even transact its authorized business. It didn't matter. The delegates understood that the national government had to be fixed. When Hamilton presumed, everyone went along. The resolution passed. Another revolution in government was underway. Because of Hamilton's illegal action, delegates met in May of 1787 to draft the Constitution.

Presumption makes revolutions. The Mashantucket Pequot tribe barely existed when Richard Hayward took over as tribal chairman in 1975. Only a handful of members lived on the remnant of tribal land, and the United States government didn't recognize them as a tribe. Hayward presumed to lead his nation anyway. After dedicated lobbying, Congress recognized the tribe and granted it sovereignty in 1983. The tribe also won an important land settlement. Hayward used the sovereignty and the money to build first a bingo hall and then the Foxwoods Casino. Hayward's presumption has made his tribe the richest in the United States.

Prepare

Plough deep while sluggards sleep.

—Benjamin Franklin

James Madison's Preparations for the Constitutional Convention

Congress agreed to Hamilton's Constitutional Convention, but directed that it be "for the sole and express purpose of revising the Articles of Confederation." James Madison had a more radical agenda. He was determined to replace the Confederation with an effective central government. Madison was not the most prestigious delegate to the Constitutional Convention, and he was painfully shy. But he was able to redirect the convention to his own program because he came prepared.

Madison spent weeks planning for the Constitutional Convention. He crafted a two-house system, modeled on Virginia's legislature. Representation was proportional, giving large states more power. And the legislature elected an executive to carry out its wishes.

Madison knew the other delegates who also supported a more ambitious constitution. He had them arrive at the convention early so he could present his ideas. Then they worked out a plan of action for moving their agenda forward. When the convention started, Madison and his allies quickly took control and their more revolutionary new government became the basis of discussion.

Preparation leads to success. Walter Chrysler was convinced that the auto industry was the future. So he borrowed a large sum to buy an expensive automobile. Then he spent the next few months taking it apart and learning how everything worked. Armed with his new automotive expertise, he won important jobs in the new industry. Soon he was running Buick for General Motors. Chrysler then turned around some struggling auto companies before introducing the first automobiles that bore his name in 1924.

Freedom of Discussion

*Every difference of opinion is not
a difference of principle.*

—THOMAS JEFFERSON

The Rules of Constitutional Convention

The Constitutional Convention began by selecting George Washington as president. Washington was a brilliant choice. He immediately gave the convention credibility with the nation, and assured that delegates would follow the rules—no one dared cross Washington. The rules for debate that the delegates adopted were just as wise.

The delegates agreed to absolute secrecy for their deliberations. Delegates could only discuss the proceedings with other delegates, and they could not give outsiders updates or progress reports. One delegate compromised secrecy by carelessly leaving documents outside of the hall. No one ever learned who the culprit was, for Washington expressed such majestic fury at the lapse that none dared admit to the error. Thereafter, all the delegates were scrupulous to preserve secrecy. Secrecy is often viewed negatively, but it was central to the success of the convention. It assured that the new constitution was debated at the convention, not in the press. Delegates raised innovative ideas without fear of public backlash.

The delegates also agreed to a parliamentary device, the Committee of the Whole. This committee included the entire convention. The Committee of the Whole would debate and agree on points, and then refer their decisions to the convention so all could debate and vote again. It seems like a clumsy arrangement, but it gave the convention enormous freedom. Delegates compromised early in the process because they knew all decisions would be revisited.

Because debate was protected by secrecy and the option to revisit decisions, the Convention made rapid progress, quickly agreeing to many vital innovations.

Innovative thinking needs to be protected and encouraged if new ideas are to flourish. Whirlpool created an internal "Innovation

Team" to keep established thinking from stifling new ideas. The group is drawn from functions and sites across the company. One of its first innovations, Inspired Chef, was a sharp deviation from its usual new products. The business unit contracts with chefs to conduct cooking classes and parties where they also sell the appliances used to make the meal. It is not the kind of idea that one would expect from an appliance company, but that is the whole point of the protected special team.

Forget Your Ego

People who are wrapped up in themselves make small packages.

—Benjamin Franklin

Madison Leads Quietly

James Madison was effective in crafting the new government to his vision largely because he did it so quietly. He kept his ego under control, coupling his wise planning with discreet politics.

Madison did not call his creation the Madison Plan. He called it the Virginia Plan. Many of the Convention's most influential delegates were from Virginia, including the convention's president, George Washington. Edmund Randolph, the respected former governor of Virginia, introduced Madison's work to the convention.

Madison shrewdly sought his ends, rather than glory or credit for achieving those ends. He was widely regarded as not only the most knowledgeable of the delegates, but also as one of the most modest. Shunning credit allowed him to skillfully craft the Constitution to an agenda he knew would work for the new nation.

Keeping your ego in check can be both productive and profitable. American Computer Hardware branched into its fast-growing storage solutions business because president Ed St. Amour was able to control his ego. One of St. Amour's employees had the idea, and rather than quash it because it didn't fit his plans for the company's printer business, St. Amour went along. The division proved so successful it was spun out as a separate entity.

Conviction

The basis of our political system is the right
of the people to make and to alter their constitutions
of government.

—George Washington,
in his farewell address,
September 17, 1796

James Wilson Demands a Strong President

Madison's Virginia Plan did not envision a strong executive, and he was not alone. Almost none of the delegates believed that the executive or executives could be anything but administrative extensions of the legislature. No one was interested in giving much power to a national leader after overthrowing a king. There were also practical problems to creating an independent executive. He would have to get his mandate someplace, and the only realistic place to get that mandate seemed to be from the legislative branch. The American people were so widely dispersed, delegates thought it impractical for citizens to elect a leader.

James Wilson, a delegate from Pennsylvania, disagreed with his colleagues. He believed it was essential that the executive's powers be separate from the legislature. His conviction eventually won over the other delegates. However, no one could think of a way to select such an executive. The convention finally agreed that each state could select electors, one for each member it had in both houses of the legislature, and the electors would select a president. Few delegates expected the electors to ever give one candidate a majority, and most of the debate centered on whether the House or the Senate would ultimately select the president. The Electoral College remains a vestige of the great confusion over how to select a president. But because James Wilson was convinced it was the right thing, the United States has a strong president who governs with a mandate from the people.

Conviction is essential to overcoming obstacles. John Bogle always believed that frugal investment management was a profitable idea. He had been convinced of this since his 1951 senior thesis. In 1976, Bogle created the Vanguard 500 Index and focused on keeping fund management expenses at a minimum. He had the numbers to prove that his index fund should give a higher return, but investors were slow to respond. For a while, index funds looked like a dead end. But Bogle was convinced index funds were the right thing to do and stuck with it. Eventually the market vindicated his conviction. Today, the index is one of the two biggest mutual funds in the United States.

Distributing Power

Give all power to the many and they will oppress the few. Give power to the few, they will oppress the many.

—Alexander Hamilton

Checks and Balances in the New Government

A key discussion throughout the Constitutional Convention was how to handle greed and ambition. The Founders assumed that whoever gained power in their new government would abuse it for their own benefit. To prevent abuse, they built checks in to minimize exploitation. They created a judicial branch that could strike down the actions of the national legislature and the executive as well as state laws. The Supreme Court was one of their most brilliant and widely copied innovations. They gave the executive a veto over legislation, and provided for the Senate to review executive appointments and treaties, and to remove the President. All were designed not for efficiency, but to diminish the abuse of power.

Madison also counted on the size and diversity of the nation to prevent abuse. Before the founding of the United States, it was widely believed that democracy would only work in small city-states.

James Madison sagely noted that the opposite was true. For all of their republican pretensions, tyrannical majorities dominated the smaller states. The diverse larger states were more democratic and better-governed.

Adding diverse points of view improves governance. George Parker had a genius for games. He loved to play, but disliked the puritanical nature of early American board games. So he sold his own game, *The Game of Banking,* which emphasized speculating and getting rich. As his business grew, Parker realized that his genius for games was not enough to run a business. He asked his brothers to join the business and oversee operations and sales while he stuck with what he did best—designing and refining the Parker Brothers collection of games.

Centralization/Decentralization

*I am more and more convinced that man is
a dangerous creature and that power, whether vested
in many or a few, is ever grasping.*

—Abigail Adams,
in a letter to her husband, John, 1775

The Role of States
The Founders didn't make the states appendages of the new Federal

government. Instead, they maintained the states' independent sovereign powers, decentralizing authority in the new nation. This decentralization is not always efficient. There are great differences in laws and procedures between states. But decentralization also fosters continued experimentation and innovation in government. State governments have pioneered reforms that later spread through the nation.

Decentralization keeps revolutions from drowning in bureaucracy. Henry Ford built the world's most successful automobile company by perfecting centralized, standardized production. But Alfred Sloan and General Motors challenged Ford's dominance by decentralizing many operations. Although not as efficient, decentralization supported innovations that allowed General Motors to surpass Ford.

Compromise

It is the trade of lawyers to question everything,
yield nothing, and talk by the hour.

—Thomas Jefferson

Overcoming the Final Hurdles

Work on the Constitution proceeded rapidly. But one critical issue remained unresolved—how to apportion power in the upper house of the legislature. Madison's Virginia Plan called for all legislative representation to be based on population, but small states feared that with proportional representation in both houses, the large states would dominate them. Delegates for the small states declared they would never support complete proportionality. Roger Sherman of Connecticut even proposed a compromise, making one of the legislative houses proportional while each state had an equal vote in the other. But Madison and other advocates of proportionality ignored their protests. They believed that anything other than strict proportionality was unacceptable.

The debate over proportionality was intense. Madison argued the correctness of proportionality point by point. Others resorted to veiled threats of sanctions and warfare if the small states didn't give in. But the impasse continued. During a caucus on July 16, Madison reviewed his options. A compromise would seriously flaw the perfection of his plan. But if he didn't compromise, there would be no replacement for the Articles of Confederation. Rather than lose the Constitution, Madison and the big states gave in. He accepted Sherman's compromise, allowing each state two seats in the upper house of the legislature. Senators were selected by state legislatures until the Seventeenth amendment to the Constitution in 1913 mandated their popular election.

> When Socal was negotiating for the Saudi Arabian oil concession in 1934, price wasn't the only issue. King Ibn Saud needed quick cash. The worldwide depression had sharply reduced pilgrimages to Mecca, the kingdom's chief source of revenue. King Saud was only considering opening his country because the need was urgent. He needed more than a fair price. He had to have it in gold, and quickly. It wasn't standard practice, but Socal realized it wouldn't get a deal unless it compromised. It agreed to Saud's terms and made the first payment with chests of gold.

Good Records

Creditors have better memories than debtors.

—BENJAMIN FRANKLIN,
Poor Richard's Almanack 1758

Records Guide the Revolution

We know much about the compromises and decisions of American Revolution and the organization of the United States government because the Founders kept excellent notes and records. John Adams requested that his wife, Abigail, keep his letters as a history of the revolution. James Madison kept a detailed account of all the discussions at the Constitutional Convention. Others kept meticulous diaries. Besides their historical value, these records proved invaluable as all of the discussions, debates, and theories were put into practice. The Founders didn't have to debate the reasons for earlier decisions. They had them in writing.

Our memories quickly distort or forget facts. A group of California undergraduates recorded detailed accounts of how and where they learned of the verdict in the 1995 O.J. Simpson murder trial. Fifteen months later, only 50 percent could accurately remember their experiences, although they had reinforced their memories by recording them. Three years later, fewer than 30 percent could correctly recall the events.

Record the reasons and results of innovative thinking. W.C. Fields stashed money all over the world in hundreds of bank accounts. Most of the accounts were in fictitious names. But Fields never recorded his aliases. He lost more than one million dollars because he forgot most of the accounts' names.

Selling Change

It is a good canvas on which some strokes only want retouching.

— THOMAS JEFFERSON

The Ratification of the Constitution

Drafting the Constitution was easy compared to selling it to the nation. For all their disagreements, the delegates to the Constitutional Convention were united in the need for a stronger national government. But most citizens were uncomfortable with the Constitution's dramatic innovations. It seemed to be headed for rejection when it was unveiled to the public.

The Constitution would never have been ratified if it hadn't been aggressively sold to the nation. George Washington was the most influential salesman. He quietly wrote state leaders in support of the new government. Benjamin Franklin gave more public support. Many citizens decided to consider the new Constitution because these trusted leaders backed it. James Madison, Alexander Hamilton, and John Jay also wrote the Federalist Papers to sell the ideas behind the Constitution. Published as a series of essays, these documents brilliantly explained how the new government would work.

However, it appeared even this persuasive campaign would not be enough to win ratification for the Constitution. Nine states needed to approve it for it to take effect. But although Delaware, Pennsylvania, New Jersey, Georgia, and Connecticut ratified quickly, supporters knew they had to win Massachusetts, Virginia, and New York, or the new government would collapse. The Constitution's backers turned their energies to winning over decision-makers in these states.

In Massachusetts, they convinced Samuel Adams to support the Constitution. Adams knew how to deliver his state. He gave John Hancock, who had not committed himself, the opportunity to offer to the state's convention a compromise of ratification with amendments. Hancock agreed, possibly because he realized that if Virginia did not ratify, he could be the new nation's first president. Without Virginia's ratification, George Washington would not have been eligible to serve as president because he would not have been considered a United States citizen. With Hancock and Adams supporting the Constitution, a number of delegates switched sides and Massachusetts ratified.

Maryland and South Carolina easily followed. Virginia and New Hampshire held their ratifying conventions next. New Hampshire became the critical ninth state to ratify on June 21. In Virginia, Edmund Randolph, a Constitutional Convention delegate who had refused to sign the Constitution, changed his mind. Although he still had strong reservations about the new government, he decided to accept it rather than risk dissolving the Union. Virginia ratified before learning that New Hampshire's approval made it the tenth state in the new government.

The New York convention began with supporters of the Constitution decidedly in the minority. New York probably would have rejected the Constitution if Virginia's approval hadn't convinced the New York convention that the Union would go on without them. Alexander Hamilton also threatened to lead the southern part of the state into the United States regardless of what the convention decided. New York reluctantly ratified. North Carolina didn't ratify until after Washington's administration began. And Rhode Island reluctantly became the thirteenth state only after the United States broke off commercial relations with it.

> Selling change is hard, even if your innovation is as brilliant as the United States Constitution. One of Sony's first products was an inexpensive tape recorder. The product was so revolutionary that no one knew what to do with it. Sony founder Akio Morita had to teach Japan how to use the innovation. With his company on the verge of collapse, he went to offices, classrooms, and parties, showing how a tape recorder could solve problems. His relentless, dedicated selling finally paid off. The recorders sold, and Sony was on its way to leading the consumer electronics revolution.

CHAPTER TWELVE

COMPLETING THE REVOLUTION

Turning Principle into Practice

On matters of style, swim with the current,
on matters of principle, stand like a rock.

—THOMAS JEFFERSON

Working Out the Details

George Washington was inaugurated the first President of the United States on April 30, 1789. For Americans, he was the only conceivable choice. However, Washington accepted only reluctantly. Alexander Hamilton and Thomas Jefferson had to persuade him to assume the arduous honor. Washington understood the difficulty of implementing the principles of the Constitution. He would need to skillfully establish precedents that reconciled the conflicting opinions about how the basic principles of the new government should be realized.

Washington's most difficult problem was his relationship with Congress. The Constitution gave him veto power over legislation but didn't specify how it was to be used. Washington had to choose between using the veto to influence the legislative process or only employing it to stop unconstitutional laws. The careful president decided to only block unlawful bills rather than interfere with the legislative branch.

However, Washington and Congress did clash over removing the President's appointees. The Senate maintained that since it confirmed them, it could remove them too. Washington won that battle. Our government would be very different if he had not prevailed.

Washington's attempt to consult with the Senate on treaties as the Constitution specified proved embarrassing. When he entered the Senate and asked for their advice, the senators had none to offer. Washington resolved thereafter to send them completed treaties, a practice that is still followed today.

> Turning principle into practice is never easy. AT&T correctly foresaw that data transmission and computers would somehow converge. It tried to put this principle into practice by buying computer and point-of-sale terminal maker NCR in 1991 for $7.4 billion. But the convergence of data transmission and computers took a different form: the Internet. The strategy failed and AT&T spun off NCR in 1996 at half its original purchase price.

Large Egos

With the same honest views, the most honest men
often form different conclusions.

—Thomas Jefferson

Washington's Cabinet

Washington became head of a government with no money, no employees, and no organization. He got his administration functioning by selecting brilliant leaders to serve in his cabinet. Alexander Hamilton headed the treasury. Henry Knox, who had led the Confederation's War Department, continued as Washington's secretary of war. Edmund Randolph agreed to serve as attorney general. And after much vacillation, Thomas Jefferson joined the administration as secretary of state.

Each appointee was highly capable and quickly organized his own department. However, his two most influential secretaries, Jefferson and Hamilton, soon quarreled over policy differences. Hamilton wanted to consolidate power, promote commerce, and look for better relations with Britain. Jefferson sought to disperse power, favored an economy of farmers, and wanted close relations with France. Their disagreements began to paralyze Washington's presidency. Jefferson became embittered and orchestrated opposition to the administration from within the government. Although Washington was able to rapidly organize a government with his brilliant Cabinet officers, melding them into a true organization proved impossible. It wasn't until Jefferson left government that Washington was able to bring peace to his cabinet.

Compatibility is as important as brilliance. When Michael Eisner recruited Michael Ovitz to join him at Disney, it seemed an unbeatable combination—bringing the most powerful man in Hollywood to its most influential corporation. But Eisner and Ovitz couldn't get along on the same team and Ovitz was gone after a year.

Reconcile

*It is easier to forgive an enemy than
to forgive a friend.*

—William Blake

Washington and Hamilton

Alexander Hamilton started the Revolution as a talented, self-taught artillery officer. His energy and talent brought him to the attention of George Washington, who made Hamilton his *aide-de-camp*. Washington relied heavily on Hamilton's organizational skills to keep the Continental Army together. But in the tension of the desperate war, Hamilton and Washington had a bitter quarrel when Hamilton was slow attending to the General. Hamilton left Washington's service.

Fortunately for the revolution, the two officers reconciled. Washington later gave Hamilton command of a New York regiment and a key assignment at Yorktown. But Hamilton's greatest contribution came as Washington's Secretary of the Treasury. America had suffered through repeated bad economic times since the start of the Revolution. Hamilton put Washington's administration and the country on a solid financial footing. He organized the Bank of the United States to facilitate federal debt issues and to create script that could be used as currency. This was especially important because Congress didn't authorize the minting of coins until 1792. Hamilton got tax revenue flowing to the new government and started the industrialization of the economy. The government and nation prospered. Washington's first administration was an economic success largely because he had the good sense to reconcile with Hamilton.

Reconciliation is good for business. Dr. John Kellogg was one of the most influential experts on health and nutrition in the United States. He had his younger brother and assistant, Will, make flakes of wheat for a healthy breakfast food. The wheat flakes were popular at the Battle Creek Sanitarium in Michigan and had great commercial promise. But the brothers quarreled over expanding the business and went their separate ways. Will switched from wheat to corn and built a lucrative cereal empire without his famous brother. Although he had pioneered a revolution in the American diet, the renowned Dr. Kellogg became a footnote to his wealthy brother because he refused to reconcile.

Private Discussions

If passion drives you, let reason hold the reins.

—BENJAMIN FRANKLIN

Financing the United States

A key element of Alexander Hamilton's financial program was for the federal government to assume state war debts. Assuming the debt would improve the nation's credit and turn the state's many influential creditors into supporters of the federal government. However, James Madison and his allies in Congress opposed assumption. The debate became so strident that it threatened the administration's financial reforms and the nation's economic health.

Thomas Jefferson was also wary of Hamilton's plan, but he realized that the nation's finances must be fixed. He ended the very public controversy with a private discussion. He had Madison and Hamilton to dinner, where they resolved the issue. Jefferson's dinner party was a complete success because he followed three basic rules for a private discussion:

➤ Invite the Right People (and Only the Right People)
➤ Have a Firm Objective
➤ Stimulate the Solution

Jefferson only invited the right people. Madison and Hamilton were the leaders of two opposing factions and could make a compromise work. Other guests were not essential and may have added complicated issues. Jefferson knew his objective— getting Madison to agree to Hamilton's plan. But Jefferson also wanted Hamilton to agree to a southern capital in exchange for Madison's concession. Finally, Jefferson was on hand to guide the discussion to its predetermined solution.

Resolve your impasse privately. J.P. Morgan worked out many difficult compromises aboard his yacht, the *Corsair*, using the same formula as Jefferson. By having the discussions at sea, Morgan easily excluded non-essential participants. He came prepared with his solution to the problem. And by detaining recalcitrant executives until they compromised, he stimulated many profitable deals.

Listen

When a man assumes a public trust he should consider himself public property.

—THOMAS JEFFERSON

Washington Takes the Pulse of the Nation

In organizing the Federal Government, George Washington faced some of the most difficult problems of any American president. He was remarkably successful in solving them because he listened to citizens. Washington held a regular levee on Tuesdays. Any polite, respectfully dressed citizen could attend. Washington did not give a speech. He just listened. He also spent many uncomfortable weeks traveling the bad roads of the new nation to meet with local leaders and citizens. Doubtless, Washington heard much that was tedious, self-serving, and useless. But listening kept Washington in touch with public opinion on what was working, and what wasn't, as he organized the new nation.

Listening is tough for revolutionaries. They are creating a brighter future and want to tell everyone about it. But revolutionaries must listen, even when they have a better idea. The Department of the Treasury has been trying for years to replace many of the one-dollar bills in circulation with coins because the bills wear out so quickly. But when Eisenhower dollars flopped and surveys found that eighty percent of Americans hated dollar coins, they ignored the feedback and produced more than eight hundred million new Susan B. Anthony coins. Predictably, the Anthony coin was another failure. Most were never circulated. But the Treasury keeps trying. We will see if the latest one-dollar coin featuring Sacagawea is more successful.

Loyalty

Labour to keep alive in your breast that little spark of celestial fire, called conscience.

—GEORGE WASHINGTON

No Help for Lafayette

The Marquis de Lafayette was the son George Washington never had. They shared a deep father-son bond that lasted throughout their lives. After Lafayette fell into disfavor during the French Revolution, he fled France and was imprisoned by Austria for five years. Lafayette and his wife appealed to Washington for support in winning his release.

Lafayette's captivity was agonizing for Washington. He desperately wanted Lafayette's success and happiness. But his paramount loyalty was to the American republic. He would not use his office as president to intervene for his friend, even though Lafayette was also America's friend. He took charge of Lafayette's son, but only with the greatest discretion. There was a real danger of war with France, and Washington was determined not to make the situation worse by antagonizing France's revolutionary government. Washington's loyalty to his nation, even at a bitter personal cost, made him the most trusted man in America.

Loyalty may be intangible, but its worth is real. A 2001 Interbrand study valued the world's top brand, Coca-Cola, at $68.9 billion. Such an asset is never free, but the result of consistent fidelity to customers and investment in superior products and services. Loyalty, or betrayal, will be remembered long after the expediency of the moment.

Trust and Authority

Unlimited power is apt to corrupt the minds of those who possess it.

—WILLIAM PITT,
BRITISH PRIME MINISTER

George Washington and Power

George Washington's incorruptible loyalty gave him unprecedented political power. Americans trusted Washington to put the needs of the country ahead of his own. During the revolution, Congress gave him almost dictatorial powers. Washington declined to use them except to show mercy to Tories. He respected other leaders, even when they were insubordinate and uncooperative. He valued subordinates, giving them the benefit of the doubt when they failed. Predictably, some people took advantage of Washington. He lost a degree of power because of it. However, this loss was more than compensated for by the whole-hearted devotion Washington earned from thousands of others.

Washington's prestige became so great that in his second term he won ratification of the hated Jay Treaty with Britain in 1794. The Jay Treaty effectively aligned the United States with Britain against France, America's revolutionary ally. The treaty was bitterly opposed by most Americans. When word of the treaty reached America, Jay was burned in effigy from Maine to Georgia. Thomas Jefferson and James Madison lined up more than enough votes in the Senate to defeat the measure. Everyone was against the treaty except for one individual: Washington.

Washington believed that America needed an alliance with Britain. The United States could not afford conflict with the Royal Navy. Anything less than peace with Britain would cripple the nation's economy. And while the Jay Treaty was advantageous to Britain, it also gave the United States what it needed.

Washington put his prestige behind the despised treaty. His stand helped some to rethink their opposition with less emotion. Others simply trusted Washington and followed him again. When the time for ratification came, the treaty was approved.

> Real authority is always derived from trust. Daimler structured its takeover of Chrysler as a marriage of equals. Then, with the merger complete, Daimler effectively took control of Chrysler. The tactic left important contributors at Chrysler feeling betrayed. Many key executives left. Those who remained

seemed to resist working for their new masters. With trust destroyed, Chrysler fell apart almost overnight. Chrysler posted huge losses and Daimler declined billions in value.

Know When to Move on

Who is wise? He that learns from everyone.
Who is powerful? He that governs his passions.
Who is rich? He that is content.
Who is that? Nobody.

—BENJAMIN FRANKLIN

A Good Revolutionary Knows When the Revolution Is Over

Samuel Adams was a brilliant revolutionary. He had few peers in exciting public opinion. We are fortunate that when his revolution succeeded, he recognized that his talent was no longer needed.

Thomas Paine was not so wise. Like Samuel Adams, he was a born revolutionary. But Paine could not stop. When the war ended, he continued directing his inflammatory rhetoric against his former comrades. Paine finally left America for Europe, where he wrote *The Rights of Man* in defense of the French Revolution and was elected to the French National Assembly. He was later thrown in prison when the political winds shifted and only barely escaped the guillotine.

Revolutions always end. When they do, revolutionaries must be prepared to move on to activities appropriate for their skills. Adams and Paine are much like two more modern revolutionaries, Henry Ford and Alexander Graham Bell. Ford insisted that the innovations he pioneered be fanatically continued regardless of the competitive environment. His inability to let go of his revolution greatly damaged the Ford Motor Company. Alexander Graham Bell realized that he was a creative genius, not a manager. Bell gracefully left his phone company to people with managerial genius. And instead of hanging around to second-guess them and undercut their authority, Bell continued to contribute outside of telephony, innovating in flight, phonographs, and hydrofoils.

Build an Organization, Not a Cult

When we assumed the Soldier,
we did not lay aside the Citizen.

—GEORGE WASHINGTON,
IN AN ADDRESS TO THE NEW YORK LEGISLATURE,
JUNE 26, 1775

Washington Retires

In 1797, George Washington made his last and perhaps most important contribution to democracy in America—he retired.

We are accustomed to peaceful transitions of power today, but in

Washington's time it was a novel idea. Leaders died or were deposed. Governance depended on one leader and faltered when he was gone.

Citizens of the infant United States thought George Washington as indispensable as any king. He was widely viewed as the only leader who could hold the country together. But Washington created a culture of leadership. Power and responsibility were distributed in his government. He counseled against putting too much trust in one leader in his farewell address. And his retirement set the precedent for the predictable changes of power. Because of Washington's wise example, the United States has avoided the disastrous leadership transitions that have plagued so much of the world.

Effective, charismatic leaders can drive organizations to spectacular success, but if a leader doesn't build a leadership team with depth and experience, the organization can fail when he departs. Rubbermaid is a perfect example. The Wooster, Ohio–based manufacturer of plastic household products, averaged an astounding 25 percent annual stock appreciation under CEO Stanley Gault. Gault made Rubbermaid one of the most admired companies in America. But without a strong culture of leadership and a CEO candidate ready for the job, Rubbermaid began foundering as soon as Gault left in 1991. Rubbermaid stock declined throughout the bull market of the 1990s until Rubbermaid was acquired in 1999 by the Newell family of companies.

New Challenges

*It is our true policy to steer clear of permanent
alliances with any portion of the foreign world.*

—GEORGE WASHINGTON,
IN HIS FAREWELL ADDRESS,
SEPTEMBER 17, 1796

War with France

On March 4, 1797, John Adams was inaugurated as the second President of the United States. Like all truly great innovations, the American Revolution was drawing to a quiet close. However, the challenges and conflicts for the new nation were just beginning.

The start of the French Revolution in 1789 first cheered and then eventually threatened Americans as France demanded that the United States support it against the monarchies of Europe. Resuming alliance with France would have been disastrous to America, but many Americans were anxious to support their former allies in their own revolutionary struggle. To them, Washington warned that alliances only last as long as common interests. In his farewell address, he cautioned the United States not to count on its allies to do anything that wasn't strongly in their own interest, and that those interests would change.

Angered at the pro-British Jay Treaty and America abandoning the French alliance, France allowed its privateers to attack American shipping. By the summer of 1797, French privateers had captured more than three hundred American ships. France also looked for territorial gains, with French spies hiring influential Americans and Canadians to support a renewed French presence in North America.

In response, the United States Navy was reconstituted. Fourteen American warships, including the USS *Constitution,* joined two hundred privateers in the undeclared war with France. The United States and Britain agreed to cooperate in the campaign, with British warships protecting both nations' Atlantic trade while the Americans guarded the Caribbean. In early 1799, the USS *Constellation* captured the French frigate *L'Insurgente,* the first of a string of impressive American naval victories. George Washington was called out of retirement to lead a new army against a feared French invasion. However, full-scale war was averted because France became too busy fighting the rest of Europe.

Objectives, alliances, and threats are always shifting. The online discount travel service Priceline tried partnering with Microsoft's Expedia to take advantage of Microsoft's expertise and clout. But after Expedia had learned how Priceline's business model operated, Expedia abandoned its partner to emphasize its own service. The problem should have been foreseen. The only thing certain about strategies and expediencies is that they will change. The next upheaval is never far away.

EPILOGUE

I will not believe our labors are lost.
I shall not die without a hope that light and liberty
are on steady advance.

—THOMAS JEFFERSON

The revolution was complete, but the American Republic was still imperfect. Most of the nation remained disenfranchised, much of it enslaved. Many still suffered from poverty, disease, and injustice. As part of their legacy of freedom, the Founders gave their heirs the opportunity of expanding freedom and prosperity through their own revolutions. Generations of revolutionaries have used that opportunity well, building a society of liberty and wealth beyond anything the Founders imagined. That legacy of constructive revolution is now ours. May we employ it with equal success.

BIBLIOGRAPHY

Revolutionary

Allen, W. B. *George Washington: A Collection*. Indianapolis, IN: Liberty Fund, 1988.

Bobrick, Benson. *Angel in the Whirlwind: The Triumph of the American Revolution*. New York: Simon & Schuster, 1997.

Butterfield, L. H., Marc Friedlaender and Mary-Jo Kline. *The Book of Abigail and John: Selected Letters of the Adams Family, 1762-1784*. Cambridge, MA: Harvard University Press, 1975.

Cappon, Lester J. *The Adams-Jefferson Letters: The Complete Correspondence Between Thomas Jefferson and John Adams*. Chapel Hill, NC: The University of North Carolina Press, 1959.

Chase, Philander D. *The Papers of George Washington: Revolutionary War Series*. Charlottesville, VA: University Press of Virginia, 1985–2001.

Collier, Christopher and James Lincoln Collier. *Decision in Philadelphia: The Constitutional Convention of 1787*. New York: Random House, 1986.

Ferguson, James (Editor). *The Papers of Robert Morris 1781–1784, Volume 4*. Pittsburgh: University of Pittsburgh Press, 1978.

Fitzpatrick, John C. *The Diaries of George Washington, 1748–1799*. New York: Houghton Mifflin Company, 1925.

Flexner, James Thomas. *George Washington: The Forge of Experience, 1732–1775*. Boston: Little, Brown, 1965.

———. *George Washington in the American Revolution, 1775–1783.* Boston: Little, Brown, 1968.

———. *George Washington and the New Nation, 1783–1793.* Boston: Little, Brown, 1970.

———. *George Washington: Anguish and Farewell 1793–1799.* Boston: Little, Brown, 1972.

———. *Washington: The Indispensable Man.* Boston: Little, Brown, 1974.

Franklin, Benjamin. *The Autobiography of Benjamin Franklin.* Boston: Bedford Books of St. Martin's Press, 1993.

———. *The Old Mistresses' Apologue: Advice to a Young Man on the Choice of a Mistress.* West Burke, VT: Janus Press, 1975.

———. *Poor Richard's Almanack.*

Jefferson, Thomas. *Jefferson Digital Archive.* University of Virginia.

Jefferson, Thomas. *The Declaration of Independence.* National Archives and Records Administration.

Lopez, Claude-Anne and Eugenia W. Herbert. *The Private Franklin, The Man and His Family.* New York: Norton, 1975.

Mansfield Jr., Harvey C. *Thomas Jefferson: Selected Writings.* Arlington Heights, IL: AHM Publishing, 1979.

Mason, George. *Virginia Declaration of Rights.* New Haven, CT: The Avalon Project at Yale Law School.

Morison, Samuel Eliot. *The Oxford History of the American People.* New York: Oxford University Press, 1965.

Morison, Samuel Eliot. *John Paul Jones: A Sailor's Biography.* New York: Time, Inc., 1964.

Paltsits, Victor Hugo. *Washington's Farewell Address.* New York: The New York Public Library, 1935.

Pararas-Carayannis, George. "Turtle: A Revolutionary Submarine." *Sea Frontiers*, July-August, 1976.

Rhodehamel, John. *The American Revolution, Writings from the War of Independence*. New York: Library of America, 2001.

———. *A New Now Age Begins: A People's History of the American Revolution*. New York: McGraw-Hill, 1976.

Smith, Page. *The Shaping of America, A People's History of the Young Republic*. New York: McGraw-Hill, 1976.

Tuchman, Barbara Wertheim. *The First Salute*. New York: Knopf, 1988.

Washington, George. *Rules of Civility and Decent Behavior*. New York: Free Press, 1997.

Withrow, Scott. "The Battle of Cowpens." National Park Service

Modern

Adler, Carlye. "The Man Who Launched 4,000 Businesses." *Fortune*, February 5, 2001.

Bailey, Jeff. "Crisis Junkie Steve Miller Thrives in His 'Corporate Salvage' Career." *Wall Street Journal*, December 16, 1997.

Banks, Howard. "Deep Stall." *Forbes*, October 29, 2001.

Barrett, William P. "The Phoenix of Phoenix." *Forbes*, January 1, 1996.

Baum, Dan. *Citizen Coors: An American Dynasty*. New York: William Morrow, 2000.

Bekier. Matthias M., Anna Bogadrdus and Tim Oldham. "Why Mergers Fail." *The McKinsey Quarterly*, 2001 Number 4.

Bell, Trudy. "The Decision to Divest: Incredible or Inevitable." *IEEE Spectrum*, June 2000

Branson, Richard. *Losing My Virginity: How I've Survived, Had Fun, and Made a Fortune Doing Business My Way*. New York: Times Business, 1998.

Brenner, Joël Glenn, *The Emperors of Chocolate: Inside the Secret World of Hershey and Mars.* New York: Random House, 1999

Brokker, Katrina. "The Best Little Oil House in Texas." *Fortune*, September 3, 2001.

Byrne, John A. "The Miracle Company." *Business Week*, October 19, 1987.

Clash, James M. "The Penny-Pincher." *Forbes*, December 10, 2001.

Colvin, Geoffrey. "How Rubbermaid Managed to Fail." *Fortune*, November 23, 1998

Conline, Rob. "Expedia Ups Ante in Priceline Patent War." *E-Commerce Times*, December 10, 1999.

Creswell, Julie. "When a Merger Fails: Lessons From Sprint." *Fortune*, April 30, 2001.

Dawson, Chester. "Saying Sayonara" *Business Week*, September 24, 2001.

Dell, Michael, and Catherine Fredman. *Direct from Dell: Strategies that Revolutionized an Industry.* New York: HarperBusiness, 1999.

Dwyer, P. "Wedtech: Where the Fingers are Pointing Now." *Business Week*, October 5, 1987.

Eisler, Kim Isaac. *Revenge of the Pequots: How a Small Native American Tribe Created the World's Most Profitable Casino.* New York: Simon & Schuster, 2001.

Fesenmaier, Jeff and Gary Smith. *The Nifty-Fifty Re-Revisited.* Claremont, CA: Pomona College online publication.

Fromson, B. D. "The Slow Death of E. F. Hutton." *Fortune*, February 29, 1988.

Giler, George. *Recapturing the Spirit of Enterprise.* San Francisco: ICS Press, 1992.

Greenfield, Jeff. "Major League Entrepreneurs." *CEO Exchange*, Public Broadcasting System, January 2001.

Greenwald, John. "The Wreck of Morrison Knudsen." *Time*, April 3, 1995

Gross, Daniel. *Forbes Greatest Business Stories of all Time*. New York: J. Wiley & Sons, 1996

Gunderson, Gerald. *The Wealth Creators: an Entrepreneurial History of the United States*. New York: Plume, 1989.

Harvard Business Review on Strategies for Growth. Boston, MA: Harvard Business School Press, 1998.

Ichbiah, Daniel. And Susan L. Knepper. *The Making of Microsoft: How Bill Gates and His Team Created the World's Most Successful Software Company*. Roseville, CA: Prima Publishing, 1991.

Johnson, Roy S. "Home Depot Renovates." *Fortune*, November 23, 1998.

Kelley, Bill. *"Whatever Happened to Run-flat Tires?" Across the Board*, May, 1994.

King, Peter. "Sudden Impact: A Megadeal sent Herschel Walker to Minnesota, where he ran wild." Sports Illustrated, October 23, 1989.

Klein, Jose. "Phil Jackson." *Salon.com*, May 29, 2001

Lewis, Tomas S. W. *Empire of the Air: The Men Who Made Radio*. New York: Edward Burlingame Books, 1991.

Mack, Toni. "Stark Raving Rich." *Forbes*, February 26, 1996.

Manes, Stephen and Paul Andrews. *Gates*. New York: Touchstone, 1993.

McLean, Bethany. "Profile in Persistence." *Fortune*, April 30, 2001.

Morais, Richard C. "Proving Papa Wrong." *Forbes*, July 9, 2001.

———. "Damn the Torpedoes." *Forbes*, May 14, 2001.

Moukheiber, Zina. "He Who Laughs Last." *Forbes*, January 1, 1996

———. "Quaker Contrarians." *Forbes*, January 22, 1996

Murphy, Victoria. "Queen for a Day." *Forbes*, July 9, 2001.

O'Brien, Jeffery M. "The Making of the Xbox." *Wired*, November 2001.

Packard, David. *The HP Way: How Bill Hewlett and I Built Our Company.* New York: HarperBusiness, 1995.

Palmeri, Christopher. "Mattel: Up the Hill Minus Jill." *Business Week*, April 9, 2001.

Pitta, Julie. "Get Smart." *Forbes*, July 9, 2001.

Reese, Jennifer. "The Man Who Couldn't Quit." *Stanford Business*, June 1998.

Rohter, Larry. "Delusions of Economic Grandeur Deep in Brazil's Interior." *The New York Times*, November 9, 1999.

Sansoni, Silvia. "The Art of Self-Promotion" *Forbes*, May 14, 2001.

Schacter, Daniel. "The Seven Sins of Memory." *Psychology Today*, May/June 2001.

Sellers, Patricia. "Get Over Yourself." *Fortune*, April 30, 2001.

Semler, Ricardo. *Maverick: The Success Story Behind the World's Most Unusual Workplace.* New York: Warner Books, 1993.

"Setting the Pace." *Technology Review*, September 2001.

Silverthorn, Ann. "Check Your Ego at the Door." *Business Solutions*, August 15, 2001.

Togo, Yukiyasu and William Wartman. *Against All Odds: The Story of the Toyota Motor Company and the Family that Built It.* New York: St. Martin's Press, 1993.

Trachtenberg, Jeffery A. "Every Decade a New Career." *Forbes*, September 10, 1984.

Useem, Jerry. "Conquering Vertical Limits." *Fortune*, February 19, 2001.

Warner, Fara. "Recipe for Growth." *Fast Company*, October 2001.

Wawro, Thaddeus. *Radicals and Visionaries: Entrepreneurs Who Revolutionized the 20th Century.* Irvine, CA: Entrepreneur Media, 2000.

Weber, Alan M. "How Business is a lot like Life." *Fast Company*, April 2001.

Wolverton, Troy. "Priceline.com Files Suit Against Microsoft." *CNET News.com*, October 13, 1999.

Yergin, Daniel. *The Prize: The Epic Quest for Oil, Money and Power*. New York: Simon & Schuster, 1991.

About the author

While in high school, Scott Thorpe built rocket and space shuttle payloads. Since then, he has designed robots and military flight simulators and launched nine major new products in companies ranging from Silicon Valley start-ups to Dow Jones Industrials. Scott Thorpe is a law student and acting CEO of transaction management startup Agincourt Systems. He combines his extensive business experience with a passion for the lessons of history. He lives in American Fork, Utah.